BEAR
WOMAN

Karolina Ramqvist is one of the most influential writers and feminists of her generation in Sweden. She has written five novels and in 2015 she was awarded the prestigious P.O. Enquist Literary Prize for *The White City*.

Saskia Vogel is a Swedish-American author, screenwriter, and translator from Los Angeles. *Permission* (2019), her debut novel, was published in five languages and optioned for television. Recently, she was awarded the Berlin Senate grant for non-German-language literature for her writing and a working grant from the Swedish Author's Fund. Her translation of Jessica Schiefauer's *Girls Lost* was a finalist for the 2021 PEN America Translation Prize and her translations of Lina Wolff and Johanne Lykke Holm have each won the English PEN Translates Award. She is a 2022 Princeton Translator in Residence.

BEAR WOMAN

Karolina Ramqvist

Translated by Saskia Vogel

MANILLA PRESS

First published in Sweden in 2019 by Norstedts
First published in Great Britain in 2022 by
MANILLA PRESS
An imprint of Bonnier Books UK
4th Floor, Victoria House, Bloomsbury Square, London, WC1B 4DA
Owned by Bonnier Books
Sveavägen 56, Stockholm, Sweden

The cost of this translation was defrayed by a subsidy from the
Swedish Arts Council, gratefully acknowledged

A CIP catalogue record for this book is
available from the British Library.

Hardback ISBN: 978–1–78658–058–0
Export ISBN: 978–1–78658–062–7

Also available as an ebook and an audiobook

1 3 5 7 9 10 8 6 4 2

Typeset by IDSUK (Data Connection) Ltd
Printed and bound in Great Britain by Clays Ltd, Elcograf S.p.A.

Manilla Press is an imprint of Bonnier Books UK
www.bonnierbooks.co.uk

'Judging from your words,' said Simontault, 'it would seem that men delight in hearing evil spoken about women, and I am sure that you reckon me among men of that kind. I therefore greatly wish to speak well of one of your sex, in order that I may not be held a slanderer by all the rest.'

'I give you my place,' said Ennasuite, 'praying you withal to control your natural disposition, so that you may acquit yourself worthily in our honour.'

Forthwith Simontault began –

'Tis no new thing, ladies, to hear of some virtuous act on your part which, methinks, should not be hidden but rather written in letters of gold, that it may serve women as an example, and give men cause for admiration at seeing in the weaker sex that from which weakness is prone to shrink. I am prompted, therefore, to relate something that I heard . . .'

Marguerite de Navarre, Tale LXVII, Heptaméron, 1559

I've realised that this story has neither a beginning nor an end. I'll write that it begins with death because it's all I'm sure of. Her father dies, and she is left alone. This is all I know.

In those early days, I would imagine a drawing whenever I thought of her. Little did I know that a drawing of her on the island did in fact exist. The one in my mind's eye was different: sloppily rendered in black ballpoint pen on a wrinkled piece of paper. It would visit me along with the thought of her – the island a crooked little circle, and alongside it a curved line marking the border between the surrounding water and the mainland.

Presumably this had to do with the incredible nature of the whole story, or at least how I interpreted it the first time I heard it. A friend had recounted it for me, a brief summary. Maybe the two of us weren't alone, but I can't remember. It's been a while now. When I look up from the computer and over at my children, fast asleep in another room while I'm out here writing this, I can tell by their faces and bodies just how many years have passed since then. I notice it every day in the words they use, the games they play and how their fingers move across their screens; and how they no longer shout when they need something, but rather they come to me.

Anyway. My friend had found this story in a book she'd had for ages, an anthology about female survivors throughout history. We were sitting in a café we used to go to, and she took it out of her overstuffed handbag and showed me. I don't remember if it was light or dark outside, and I don't remember what I said or thought right then. My memory is unreliable, and I think this applies to others' too – we remember what we want to remember, as we want to remember it, and allow ourselves to forget the rest. We forget the people who aren't important to us, we forget things we've done and said that other people will remember forever, and we forget what others have said and done to us.

I remember my friend talking about Marguerite de la Rocque, but I don't think she was calling her by name – the name I would give her myself didn't come to me until later, when I was walking home through the snow. I remember looking down at the table between us, at the cups and water glasses and phones we'd put there. Thinking about it now, it's possible that one of us might have taken a paper and pen and sketched out the island and its geographical location on earth, or perhaps that drawing had never existed. I could have constructed my memory of it in retrospect. Maybe it was there on the table, maybe not, but for a long time that drawing was the first thing I saw when I thought of Marguerite, before what was in my mind's eye became a kind of representation of reality – as I was imagining reality had been before I started on this: the island and its surroundings, with its vast estuary which then, as now, was known for being the largest on earth. And beyond it the ocean, landmasses and frozen seas, all the other islands and islets freezing together during the winters, where there was no one else around for thousands upon thousands of miles. Endless white vistas as barren and empty as the rest of that part of the world, stretching from Mexico to Alaska, a vast continent spanning tens of thousands of miles from north to south and east to west – populated by one single solitary human.

Or so it has been described.

Later, I stood in the snow at the crossing on our street as the traffic thundered past, the wide twin pram like a nylon and black plastic ship in front of me. It was snowing, but the weather hadn't quite hit yet. It was barely below zero that day and yet I was freezing. It was as though the cold were coming from within, as though my very flesh were deep frozen. Recently I'd noticed that I no longer had any defence against the cold and the dark that autumn had laid across our part of the north and which lingered from winter far into spring.

My son was a little over one year old, and his sister, lying beside him in the pushchair, was only a few months. My oldest daughter had just started school. I was thirty-five. In some ways, my having three children was cause for surprise. I was often asked how it felt and what it was like to have had two kids in such quick succession, and mostly I'd say it was easy. I think I'd say this because it was actually how I saw it; perhaps the love I felt for these children had made me unable to see my reality for what it was. But I know I harboured a wish for it to be easy; a notion that it had to be, that I wasn't

allowed to cast a shadow on what should be light: creating
new life, another person's existence.

The cold and dark were entrenched inside me, and they
intensified each other. It felt cold in the flat as well, because
the heating system in our building couldn't really keep
up when the temperature dropped. The constant freezing
paired with the lack of daylight fatigued me. Every day I was
utterly exhausted, even though I'd hardly exerted myself.
I wore thick sheepskin slippers around the apartment and
wherever I sat down to read or write or breastfeed my
youngest daughter there were blankets to wrap myself in;
when I went out I wore woollen long johns under my regular clothes and a horrible ankle-length down coat I'd bought
cheap online. Still I couldn't keep warm.

I found out it had to do with my endocrine system, a gland
that influenced my metabolism and a bunch of other processes
and which could cause any symptom at all, really, if it was
off-kilter. The doctors at the hospital said it was harmless and
very common among working women my age with young
children. It was common for it to get worse after multiple
pregnancies, difficult or back-to-back births; it was common
for it to get worse if there were several children in the family;
and the condition could be further exacerbated by trauma and
stress. All you could do was take the prescribed pills and try to
minimise strain, physical as well as mental.

I didn't know how that was supposed to happen.

The children were tucked into their padded pushchair muffs, silently gazing into the black afternoon sky. The sky was so deep and unreachable it made me think of space, which was up there somewhere as I was down here looking up at it while waiting for the light to turn green – looking up so that I could see what they were seeing from the pushchair, and because I liked the idea of glimpsing the infinity that begins not far from here.

The crossing light turned green. All I had to do was cross the street, then we'd almost be home, but I didn't have it in me. I couldn't take another step through the slush with that wide carriage. I thought of the entrance to the bicycle room around the corner from our front door, where the pushchair had to be stored due to fire safety regulations; it was an iron door almost entirely covered in graffiti, and when I caught sight of it, I could already feel its weight against me. I could see myself trying to open the door and then hold it open to get the pushchair into the corridor, which was so narrow that I'd have to back out again if someone came walking from the other direction. I would unsnap the five-point harnesses and pick the children up so that I could guide the pushchair into the pushchair area, which had recently been built as there were so many small children in the building, so many couples in their thirties buying apartments, moving in and making babies as soon as they arrived. We'd done that too.

People made their way across the road. Bicycles, push-chairs, dogs. I stayed put. I imagined us going up to the apartment. I would sit down on the kitchen stool and start nursing, then I'd consider finding a more comfortable seat so that my body wouldn't end up aching, but I wouldn't have the energy to shift my position or relocate; my husband would come home from work or maybe from the Irish pub that used to be in our neighbourhood – it had been there as long as I could remember but it's not anymore – and we would change the children and bathe them in the plastic tub on the shower floor and try to fit in making dinner and maybe tidy up the apartment a bit, and then we'd read or watch TV and the day would be over and night would arrive, followed by another day, and I'd have to go out and do it all again, and it would go on like this, because yet another day would follow, and then another, filled with the same things.

I stayed put, watching everyone else pass by. I let go of the pushchair and took my phone out of my pocket and dialed my husband's number. He answered right away and I asked him where he was. Then I waited until he came and took the pushchair and together we crossed the street and entered the building.

From that day on I couldn't stop thinking about her. This period now seems almost like a delimited space in time, those first years with a husband and three children – and her entry into my life right then. It wasn't so much the thoughts in my head – they weren't particularly developed as far as I recall – but more how I pictured her. She seemed so close, as though she and I were in the same room, as if that distant place were materialising here: her body clad in bearskin and a tattered, high-necked dress; or naked, her skin's every extravasation exposed, beaten, dirty and blushing, pale against the darkness, the ground, the mountain and earth.

The feeble daylight can't reach her where she lies inside the cave. I think she would have wished for no one to find out about it, about '. . . *a life under extrinsic conditions no better than an animal's* . . .', yet I write that she's in there. Now I either picture her in this darkness or in the wide expanse of time and our shared history, the vast nothingness from which she emerges – only to be consumed by it again.

A ndré Thevet first mentions her in the twenty-third part of *La Cosmographie Universelle* (a book intended to describe every part of the then-known world) from 1575. Page 1,019. By first name only: *Marguerite*. There aren't many other details about her given. Not when or where she was born nor who her parents were, even though he most probably knew, because even though she's a woman, she's still an aristocrat. Even where she ended up after it was all over is only hinted at by his naming of the village where he meets her:

> . . . *the village of Nautron, country of Périgord, at which time I was with her and she made ample discourse with me of this misadventure and of all her past fortunes.*

This is Elizabeth Boyer's translation. Thevet wrote 'Nautron', but according to Boyer there has never been a village in France with that name. Like several other historians, she concludes that it refers to Nontron. Thevet must have spelled it wrong, but I wonder if he didn't do it on purpose, to camouflage the place name from the reader.

None of the sources reveals much about her life before or after these events. It's as though she's only present in their accounts – accounts that had not, in the first instance, been authored for her sake, I thought, but for the sake of the story itself: its scientific or literary value and how it could serve the writer. At least, this was my first take.

Everybody said it was a fantastic story, and such comments always provoked a reluctance in me. They made me question things: my motives and what actually attracted me to the story – I, who had never been partial to fantastical narratives and who was so tired of stories. I was *still* tired of stories. I reviled them for how they seemed to be impacting the world; for how the telling itself seemed to have become everything, whereas truth and silence were nothing anymore.

Maybe this is nothing new. Maybe people have always felt this way. As I'm writing, it's even clearer to me how fiction – or a sort of fictive sheen – guides our thoughts and conceptions and sets events in motion. If someone had told me as a young author that this was how it would go, I would have probably thought I'd find a way to make peace with it, but I haven't. I'm simply afraid. It's like witnessing a stubborn storm rumbling in, the violent power of story crushing everything in its path and dragging it along. Bit by bit what was once my world has vanished and has been refashioned as a new reality, partly inscrutable to me, in which I question the validity of what, until recently, I trusted.

My computer's desktop wallpaper is a photo of the tower in Roberval. It isn't one of the many pictures I took when we were there last summer, but one I downloaded from the web, showing the place in autumn, the leaves on the large trees luminous orange and muted brown. Bare, black branches like thick strokes of ink reach for the white sky and the lawn is only visible in patches, its once vibrant green faded and dull. My documents are scattered across the image, obscuring it at random. Most of them only contain a sentence or two: a note, or one of my many attempts to start something new.

Something other than this.

I've hardly looked at my own pictures in the year since our afternoon by the chateau, but I also have in my possession a tiny souvenir. It is a parcel made of dried leaf, no larger than my palm, brittle and perforated from holding it and looking at it whenever I need a break from this project. (I've learned that taking breaks helps.) Only the leaf's slender veins are intact and still clinging to its contents, which are almost completely unprotected now.

I TRIED TO work on this, my own account, every day that autumn and throughout the prolonged period of darkness that has since passed. Even though I couldn't, I persisted. (My inability is becoming so clear to me as I go through what I've written. All these things that I've realised have to be noted down and must come out along with everything else.)

Not having writing at my disposal was highly unusual for me. I had it and yet I did not. It wasn't really available to me anymore. As soon as I hit a hurdle, which was constantly, because that's what it is to write, at least for me, my attention splintered, thoughts slipped away and vanished. I drifted from the subject; my mind took me from the place in the text where I needed to be to somewhere simpler and more pleasant, like our last morning in Paris and the memory of who I had been then, when I still had some sort of confidence in things.

After I'd made my attempts at writing, on some days I'd sit with the computer at an old bureau I'd moved from our bedroom into the hall when the daylight hours were shrinking and the darkness entering the apartment made it hard to write. I thought it might be easier there. When I found the drawing of her on the island that Thevet had used to illustrate a chapter about her in *La Cosmographie Universelle*, I printed it out and pinned it to the wall. It's a murky image, an etching, reproduced in the book in the middle of a gorgeous spread: dense lines of his writing, blackened columns

and their ornamental initials, marginalia, and the short itali-
cised caption.

I'd stuck other pictures to the wall as well, but I didn't look
at them as often. It was the etching to which my eyes were
drawn, a particular point on it, a small oblong shape on the
left. Now I know what it represents, but back then it was still
indecipherable.

I write that it begins with death, and it is her father who dies. She's looking down into the pit that will be filled with earth from the pile beside it. The gravedigger and the men who carried the coffin all the way from the village are waiting in the distance. They're looking at each other or away, hiding their eyes, as though one glimpse of her would infect them with her pain. They are dressed in the simple dark garments characteristic of their kind. At dawn they walked between the forest and the black fields, carrying the coffin along the clay path that leads far beyond the village, to the secluded resting place for their dead.

I write that she is alone at the open grave. Is she alone, or is Damienne already with her?

Damienne is charged with looking after her: it's her duty, but when the task was assigned, and by whom, cannot be known. Nothing can be known about this beginning, except this death. It is sure and certain. A father dies, and she is left alone.

Had she not been orphaned while still a minor, the king would not have appointed Roberval as her guardian and what would later happen would never have happened. I would never have found out that someone like her existed. The days and hours I've spent with this would have been passed otherwise.

Of Sieur Jean-François de la Rocque de Roberval much is written. It wasn't long before I knew each of his names and titles, his parents' and relatives' names and titles, the names of the men who have written books and articles about him and about everything named after him, including the high school in Montréal and the small city outside Québec. The latter is now best known for an open-air swimming competition on a thirty-kilometre stretch across the Lac Saint-Jean and for an NHL match between the Montréal Canadians and the Buffalo Sabres having been played there in 2008. I read about his family's connections to various events in the religious conflicts that were splintering Europe at that time, the start of what has been called the Age of Exploration, and I read that as a child he'd become rather close friends with François d'Angoulême, the prince later crowned François I, the great king who would unite the country and create modern France, and who I, without really meaning to, would find out more and more about over the course of this project.

In an image folder on my computer, I'd saved a portrait of Jean-François de la Rocque de Roberval drawn by the court painter Jean Clouet in 1540, when Roberval was forty years old. It's part of the Musée Condé's collection of depictions

of François I and his inner circle. When you google Roberval many versions of it appear, edited and colour-graded
in various ways, but the original is drawn in red chalk, as
portraits were during the Italian Renaissance, a stylistic
period held in high esteem by the court. Jean-François de
la Rocque de Roberval sports a beard and moustache and
his hair curls at his temples. He has defined cheekbones
and a long nose, and yet the face gives a somewhat blunt
impression, more rough-hewn than noble, if faces can
even be discussed in such terms. His gaze is fixed in the
distance, at once steady and melancholic, and even though
I can't see his full figure, my guess is that he's short and has
large, wide hands. This is the year before he receives his
colony-command mandate from the king and presumably
also before he receives her. As her guardian, he was to take
responsibility for her until she reached the age of majority
for women, which was then set at twenty-five, or until the
day she entered into another man's possession (or should I
write 'protection'?) through marriage.

I don't know how long she waits for him to arrive, but I'll write that it's winter. It is the winter of 1541 somewhere in southern France, where families had built their castles on the mountain rock – 'de la Rocque'. The hillside is steep and rocky and she makes her way up and over it. The clay has turned the yellow grass from the year before grey and on the slope, between tufts and stones, lie pale stripped sticks, which she collects and carries to the castle.

She's in the middle of the courtyard when she hears them: his horse's hooves on the frozen ground. I write that they load his carriage with her personal effects and other items from home, then they take their seats next to each other inside its darkness, and that the movement of the carriage bumping along the wheel ruts glittering with frost relaxes her. As does the relief of him finally having fetched her.

They sit in silence and after an hour or so she dozes off, asleep and in slumber, her head resting on him, mouth open, drool travelling down her chin. He looks straight ahead and his gaze reveals nothing about his intentions, what he means to do now that he has collected her.

But all of this is just an image of gentility from bygone eras, easy to visualise. I'd seen it before, a man and a woman sitting like that in a carriage. I wanted to know what carriages from the early 1540s looked like, but my research showed that they weren't common in France back then. They were in fact the height of luxury; in the entire country, there were only three carriages, and they all belonged to the royal stables. Even if Jean-François de la Rocque de Roberval was one of the king's closest friends, she wasn't likely to have been important enough for him to have borrowed a carriage in order to collect her. Or was she? Most seem to think it unlikely, considering what is known about the events to come, and what she did.

Me, I was going to write a feature film based on her story. Like many others I'd noted that so-called historical dramas were often about privileged lives, incomparable to those of the vast majority, but when I started writing and tried to find out more about this period and about her, I realised how hard it would be to resolve it any other way. The lives of kings and queens were those that reached through the centuries because they were the ones written into history, art and culture, but also because they had what others did not.

Carriages, politics, the written word.

Again and again I found myself having depicted events and situations that I had to change because I realised they required her to hold a very high status. Time after time I managed to draw the royal family into the action somehow.

Most of all I was fascinated by the relationship between the king and his sister – who was also named Marguerite, and whom he called *la marguerite de marguerites*, the marguerite of marguerites, and who would later become better known by her regnal name of Marguerite de Navarre. Their mother, Louise de Savoie, believed in equality between the sexes and had given the two siblings the same high level of education. Their father had died when they were four and two years old, after which Louise, who was then nineteen, is said to have dedicated all her energy to providing her children with the best possible schooling and to strengthening the family's influence. She called it *notre trinité,* our Trinity. In this constellation each and every position was dependent on the other, and each action was carried out with the intention that François would grow up to be the king of France. Mother and sister had to do everything in their power to achieve this goal. They had to support and elevate him in all respects, guide him while making sure he felt omnipotent.

I liked reading about these lives and how they related to each other and to various ideas about how the world was made and how countries and people should be governed. There was plenty written about the royals and their inner circle. But my interest in this ran counter to my other strong desire: finding out how it all 'really' was. It was unlikely that the Marguerite I was in the process of discovering would have come from a very rich and genteel family, considering what would happen to her, how she and those surrounding her handled it, and the fact that she managed to disappear afterwards, that her existence has been erased.

I spent a lot of time hunched over my computer looking at pictures, oil paintings and sketches of people from back then. There was a certain unexpected pleasure to it, seeing them lined up on the screen; their facial features, the nuances of colour, the shimmering light in the artworks that seemed so advanced and must have taken ages to render. It calmed me somehow. I went through countless portraits of young women who I thought might have been around her age to see how they were dressed and what they looked like. Their airs and expressions. Sometimes names and years were given. I read up on the items of clothing I could see – a white collar and a small hat called a French bonnet – although sometimes I read about the garments first, then studied the portraits to see how they were portrayed. I looked at the castles and the royal hunting grounds, at older women and noblemen.

Later, when I'd learned a bit more about the French Renaissance, my perception changed; but there, in the beginning, the time during which this story took place seemed empty. However entranced I was, the period seemed almost worryingly devoid of content and shrouded in darkness, like it had nothing whatsoever in common with my own time. It wasn't just the lack of carriages, it was the lack of everything. Everything seemed to have arrived later, everything seemed to have happened later. I took every opportunity to work the 1500s into conversation so that I could find out what others imagined it to be like or their thoughts on the period, but in my follow-up research, it turned out that what people usually referred to had happened later, in the 1600s, or earlier, during the Middle Ages.

I became increasingly convinced that it wasn't out of the ordinary for something like this to have happened back then; not in light of what I was learning about how people's lives were – driven by a sort of chance-based, obliterating darkness controlled by nothing but the maxim that only the fittest survive. Personal gain seemed to have been everyone's lodestar, quite simply because life was hard, so hopeless and utterly unpredictable. The ideals of the Enlightenment and of democracy had started to take shape, but autocracy and religion, magic and mob rule still dominated. All in all, this made me feel insecure at first, thinking about how difficult it would be to portray an event that took place in such a wretched era, so far from the comforts I knew. But with time this changed, and now the world she lived in doesn't seem as foreign anymore. Its brutality doesn't seem as singular and mysterious as it once did.

My own father had died as well. It wasn't exactly a sign, not like the other signs, but I can see how it was also a beginning for me. Presumably *when* my father died had a lot to do with it, as it happened the very day my son was born. It was so overwhelming. I think this must've been what caused the state I found myself in ever since, and which I'd like to believe is in the process of dissolution. But is it really?

I imagined that she and her father were close. They must've been, since she could read and write. If he allowed her to get an education, in spite of her being a woman, then he must have held her in some sort of regard. He must have loved her, or at least felt a sense of responsibility for her. Perhaps he harboured hope for what she could make of her life.

My own father had always been absent and unreachable, but when he unexpectedly ceased to exist, it was too much for me. I so clearly remember holding my newborn son to my chest and the telephone to my ear while listening to the message saying he was gone, but the time that followed is veiled in shadow. My memories are so few. People often bring up events from those first years, evenings or days we spent together, which I don't remember. Thinking about it now, it's like I've just woken up from a deep sleep and am looking around at everything that happened while I was gone. It's difficult for me to comprehend how so much time could have passed with me hardly noticing. The children have become so big. It's easier now that we don't have to drag them along in the pram, carry them, change them, feed and lull them, and hold them tightly so they feel safe enough to sleep.

But other things are, of course, more difficult now.

Most of what I remember is related to their bodies: them falling ill or hurting themselves, their milk bottles and dummies, them getting dandruff and threadworm, and how their flesh felt in my hands, their skin against mine. I remember my own body as a discarded casing and I remember rubbish bags full of leftovers and soiled nappies sitting by the door because we didn't have time to throw them away or couldn't carry them to the waste disposal downstairs while also carrying the children.

In my pictures from that time, we're lying on the bed or on the sofa – a gigantic sofa we'd bought, which was big enough for all of us to sit on, reading and watching TV in the evenings like you imagine families do – and the children are on and around me. I'm holding the telephone overhead, afraid of dropping it on one of them, afraid of hurting them with it or with what was inside me. I took lots of pictures, as parents do, to catch the passing moments, but also to confirm that, yes, I was actually there. My oldest daughter is either looking at me or her siblings or into the camera and smiling; the smallest one is lying on an old patterned blanket we'd found out in our country cottage and brought home; and their brother is laughing and jumping around right next to them. I remember fearing he'd accidentally jump on his little sister, or that that's what he wanted to do, and I remember being anxious about my oldest daughter feeling left out because her younger siblings were taking up so much of my time. I didn't know how I was supposed to ever be enough.

During this time I often thought of the cave: her crawling inside it and lying down. Her face against the mountain rock, half hidden by her hair. The silence and darkness in there.

My constant worry was like a wind coursing through the rooms of our apartment, refusing to leave me as long as I was present. I wanted to protect the three of them all of the time: from each other, from us, from everything, as I'd wanted to protect myself. My entire life I'd been fearful and had worried about all sorts of things. I'd been afraid of existing at all, but I'd done everything I could to suppress that fear. With three children this was no longer possible. What I'd been afraid of seemed even more frightening now, and being alone didn't mean what it used to. I would quite simply never be alone again, because I would always have them. This is what I was thinking and there was no comfort in the thought. All it was to me was dark – their lives depending on me.

Later I would consider the alternative and know it to be worse. I'd always done everything I could to protect myself from other people, fend off their advances and get myself to a place where I could be all alone.

I didn't google her right away. I didn't do anything with her name when I first heard it. All I wanted was to hold on to the images of her that had arisen in me. They perforated my muffled reality: brief dreams wedged into my mind. Her body, the island, the animals emerging from the forest. In those early years, with a growing family, she seemed to be sending flashes of light through the darkness of my existence, a darkness almost as dense as the past: what lay behind me and what lies behind us all, all that we share.

I liked the nights I spent discussing her with my friend at the café and I liked how she kept working her way into my fantasies. Maybe I thought I was betraying her by becoming yet another person who was choosing to turn her life into yet another representation. 'Life' is saying a lot, of course; I mean the events which have led to us knowing that someone like her was once alive.

Her story bore witness to something related to me somehow and I couldn't let it go. I also kept finding myself wondering about the pull her story had on me and feeling almost ashamed of it. For various reasons.

The very thought of her existence comforted me, and at first I was reluctant to find out more in case I might spoil it. I wrote a film treatment based on her story as I understood it, and after submitting it I waited around for a long time for the script to be commissioned.

While waiting, I kept trying to go back to my novel, which I'd set aside to work on the film, but I couldn't. I was still thinking about her every day. There was no room for anything else.

In some sense I'd always been reluctant to do research for fear it might lead to revelations that would spoil the writing process for me, and that my loyalty to the real would prove greater than my loyalty to the work. Of course I took reality into consideration – however I felt or thought about it, it breezed in and out of me – but I didn't want to end up in a situation where I felt compelled to subordinate myself to it. Maybe I hadn't yet understood what writing is – that it, like all narration, implies a forceful takeover. And whoever I was and however I felt, I was still a writer, describing other people and the world, thereby owning them in the way that language and stories had always owned me.

So Jean-François de la Rocque de Roberval comes riding to the castle – no carriage – and they must have ridden away from there together, strapping her luggage to the horses' backs and setting off. The village notary compiles an inventory of everything they take with them. Before they leave, he hands it to her and asks for her seal, but because she can write she takes out an inkwell and quill and signs her name along the bottom of the page – which will disappear, along with everything else to do with her.

After this she visits her room. There she retrieves her book and wraps it up in her hair, fixing it in place with long pins. That's how light and small the book is. They go out to the courtyard together, and she mounts her horse in the only way women were allowed – not in a saddle but on a narrow platform with a ledge for her feet – and they take the path that runs down one side of the mountain. She looks back at the castle up high, as pale as the mountain, but like an outcrop on the side of it. They ride along rocky paths, scores and scores of kilometres through the same terrain, past burning villages and abandoned ones. Robbers

and bandits approach but veer off at the sight of him: a cor-
sair, a heavily armed captain, a viceroy-to-be.

After that evening and night and another day and night, the
tower appears. He has had it erected near the south-western
part of the low stone wall surrounding his castle. This is his
creation. Though it is not his first time seeing it from the narrow mud tracks running across the hills on the south side, the
full force of the sight is undeniable: the tower is higher than
the castle itself, octagonal, with windows to the east and south
on both floors, and a pointed roof upon which sits a belfry. To
crown the belfry, he commissioned an ornament in the shape
of a cube with four grimacing faces, each facing one of the
four cardinal points. On top of the cube is a dove perched on
a sphere. The sculpture is small, but it has a refined Venetian
elegance that calls to mind travel, science, exploration. The
man he has been and the one he will become.

All he wishes shall come to pass.

But 'wishes' probably isn't quite the right word. I don't
think he wishes things into being: he commands them.

'As far as the ill-fated nièce Marguerite is concerned the papers
hold their tongue,' wrote M. l'Abbé Émile Morel and Henri Le
Fèbre in September 1892, after they'd both gone through the
archives at Château de Roberval. All documents concerning
her have been destroyed.

Thevet describes it in this way too: Jean-François de
la Rocque de Roberval was her uncle, but according to

Elizabeth Boyer he couldn't have been because she was
neither his sister's nor his brother's child. (His brother was
a priest.) It is likely that she was his cousin. Ill-fated she
was without a doubt. But can you really say that? Was the
ill that befell her fated?

Jean-François de la Rocque de Roberval never married,
even though marriage was at that time, in principle, obliga-
tory for men of his status. As such, there has been specula-
tion, as it is often called, about the nature of his sexuality and
his relationship to women. André Thevet, as well as his biog-
rapher, Robert de la Roquebrune de la Roque, describe him
as a kind of playboy who, in the years before everything that
happened, lived a rakish life at court, amassing large debts,
while allowing the king and everyone else to believe his fortune was intact. He had borrowed money against several of
his assets, but with the tower he would be able to take out
new loans. He also had a church built in the village – whether
this was for economic reasons or because he wanted to serve
God, or both, seems unclear, and is of course impossible to
say with any certainty – but it was commissioned after he'd
heard he was being considered for a mission for the Crown
that might solve all of his problems.

When I saw the tower for myself, it seemed small, which I suppose is often the case with things you've only ever seen in pictures or read or heard about. And yet it had a pull on me. It was the most phallic building I'd ever seen, so firmly ensconced in aggression and a steadfastness that seemed to draw me in like a magnetic field. It radiated raw masculine energy – but did it really, or did I just think it did because I knew who built it?

My oldest daughter was the same age as I had been the first time I visited Paris, and I'd decided to take her for a long weekend. The explicit reason was my research for the script I was to write. I wanted to see Roberval's tower and visit Place Joachim du Bellay, a square in Paris connected to him and so, of course, to her.

But there were other, cloudier, reasons.

I had so longed to return to Paris after not having been for years, and once I'd had the idea of going with my oldest daughter, I couldn't let it go. The idea was burdened by the guilt I felt for wanting to leave the quotidian behind – my husband and the little ones – for several days. But the little ones weren't so little anymore, it wouldn't be too taxing for my husband to be alone with them and, anyway, with all my work trips in recent years, both he and they were used to me being away.

Then there was my curiosity. I was keen to know what my daughter would make of Paris, and I also wanted to know if it was true that the city's conservatism had kept it alive for its visitors – that it remained a vibrant city at a time when other cities mostly felt like shopping centres for international travellers. Paris was still itself, it was said.

When planning the visit, I'd initially thought our first stop would be Roberval, in the neighbouring district of Oise. We'd get that trip out of the way so that we could enjoy the weekend. But then I thought what a shame it would be to miss Friday in Paris and that I'd rather pass through the village on the way home on Monday, when much would be closed and the city less interesting.

I'd seen the grey tower in books and on one of the websites I had been browsing in the evenings when the children were sleeping and my husband was on the sofa reading or watching TV. On one page about French castles it said that Château de Roberval was privately owned and not open to visitors. This didn't really matter to me, as the original castle inhabited by him – and presumably her, at least briefly – was destroyed by a fire and what was there now had only been built in 1784, more than 200 years after his death. There was no need to visit the castle or find out who the current owner was. And yet there was something about the sentence: *le chateâu ne se visite pas* – as though it contained a message for me. As though something, or someone, was trying to keep me from what I was looking for – whatever that was.

A mighty heatwave had just swept in across southern Europe, with temperatures measuring higher than at any other time in the past century. People had even died in the heat. There was talk of climate change, as there had been for many years, but now the discussion was whether this heatwave proved we were already suffering the environmental consequences faster than anyone could have imagined, or if it would turn out that the extreme weather was nothing but a blip. There were also people who'd begun to assert that the theory of global warming was a modern myth, questioning the very existence of climate change, its impact on the planet, on nature, and its threat to the continued existence of the species.

When we arrived in Paris, heat still blanketed the city. I'd booked us into a cheap hotel in the northern part of the medieval Latin Quarter. We took the metro from the airport bus station by Porte Maillot and went straight to lunch at an old bistro I've always liked on Rue de Bretagne, which had become the kind of place where people made videos and took pictures of themselves for Snapchat, Instagram or other social media. When we took our seats on the patio, I noticed that my daughter was noticing the same things that I had when I was her age. The city I had known was still there, in the music coming from the cars and the zip of the Vespas zigzagging between them, in the way people moved and in everything else we could see and hear.

It wasn't her first visit to Paris, but I think it was her first time seeing it in this way. After a second she went quiet and seemed conscious of her movements. She stole glances at the women sitting around us and then turned to me and said I could smoke if I wanted to.

I'd hidden my smoking from her, in part because of the vaguely formulated idea that a mother shouldn't smoke in front of her children, as to a child's eyes it's something lethal, but now that she was older she'd caught me in the act more than once and I'd admitted to having the odd cigarette when she wasn't around.

'I don't mind if you do it while we're here,' she said.

I took my cigarettes out of my bag and wondered if she'd seen the packet in there.

My daughter kept her eyes on the street life. Her reactions revived me. What a relief to discover that certain moods could still only be experienced in certain places, and that there was still such a thing as feeling a 'sense of place'. Recently, I hadn't been so sure. My trips had been surprisingly stimulating as far as work was concerned, speaking about my books, meeting other authors and participating in discussions and readings, but when I was left to my own devices to explore, with only a phone as my guide, I was often plagued by the sense that the world I was travelling around in wasn't ours, but rather a digital representation of it, and as such billions of different worlds. This seemed to nullify travelling as a phenomenon, or at least compromise its most fundamental qualities. My travelling companions and I would walk between the sights and restaurants and famous addresses and geo-tag ourselves, barely glancing at anyone around us because, instead, we were waiting for reactions from people we already knew and our followers on social media.

In Paris there were no known traces of Marguerite de la Rocque, if that even was her last name. Indeed, Paris was near to Roberval, but the court kept to Château d'Amboise, the enormous castle built sometime in the 1000s on a spur above the River Loire and which, in olden times, had acted as a Gallic-Roman fortification. It is impossible to know if she'd ever been to Paris, but everything I saw seemed to remind me of her. Rue de Bretagne; Rue de Saintonge; the medieval quarters, whose pale buildings were another reason why I'd chosen our hotel: of all the physical objects in the world that were somewhat within my reach, these were among the few that had existed when she had. I tried to imagine what the oldest buildings had been like when she'd have looked up at them, as we were doing, towards their roofs and the sky above.

Those neighbourhoods were now cosy and chic; they'd developed into the kind of places where weekend tourists like us wanted to hang out. We ate at cafés that, to the best of my knowledge, had never not been there. They looked the same as they always had and were now considered symbols of something more authentic than anything new. We walked the streets I'd often walked when I was my daughter's age; she asked me what the area used to be like, which was something I had been thinking about too – what it had been like to move through the city as a teenage girl, as a young woman. As I write this, I notice I still want to protect myself from the latter description and I wonder if a language exists in which those words are not poisoned, in which the person to which they refer is entirely unproblematic.

I had considered visiting Chantilly to look at Jean-François de la Rocque de Roberval's portrait, but now that we were finally in Paris and only had the weekend, it didn't seem important. The portrait of François I, however, which hangs in the Louvre and is thought to have been painted by the same artist – that I wanted to see. It's an example of Mannerism in the paintings from the early 1500s that I'd been looking at. It would call to me in the mornings as I sat with my computer in the kitchen's twilight before having to drop the children off. I'd enjoyed studying it while waiting for them to get ready: the depth of the image on the screen, the king's pale skin and the rich scarlet brocade woven with crowns behind him, the glossy satin rippling from his unnaturally broad shoulders. I absolutely wanted to see it in the Louvre. This would work out well, because my daughter was set on seeing the Mona Lisa, *La Joconde.*

On our way, we walked through the Tuileries and the amusement park that is now there in the summer.

'Can't we go on a ride?' my daughter asked, pointing at the largest attraction, a giant sheet-metal monstrosity with music jangling from the speakers and long swings in which people had just started to take their seats. She looked longingly at the contraption, then back at me. 'Just one ride?'

The fact was, we were pressed for time because the museum was closing at 6 p.m., and it was now 4.30, but I said OK, climbed the steps and paid the cashier.

My daughter followed, displaying exaggerated surprise, but also amusement, saying that never in a million years had she thought I'd say yes.

We sat down in one of the swings, while two men speaking in what sounded like Polish went around lowering and tugging at the safety mechanisms. Then one of them pushed a large button that set the carousel in motion. The machine rattled into action, rising and falling, only to rise again. We were hoisted gradually, swinging higher and higher in the hot July air, and when we were all the way at the top, we looked down at Paris: the inner-city neighbourhoods, spreading north and then out in every direction, the far river bank, the avenues of trees and the pale gravel paths in the park and the ponds where remote-controlled sailboats moved around. We flew sideways, high above it all, laughing and screaming and clinging to each other. Deep down, my daughter wasn't afraid, neither of speed nor heights. As for me – I'd never dared go on rides, not even as a child, perhaps not least because I was the kind of child who saw the danger in everything. Now, I was enjoying the feeling. It was like being freed from myself, and it embarrassed me slightly to know she could see it too.

I kept hold of my phone as we left the park for the enormous palace that lay between us and the river. While waiting for traffic to pass and then crossing the street, I was googling the Louvre so that I could tell her something about it, something more than I already knew, and the search result that first caught my eye was this: the king who'd converted the medieval fortress that had stood there into the Renaissance palace the Louvre is today was François I. He'd made it his temporary residence in Paris, I read, and had given the art he collected there and at his other castles to the French state.

Because it was late in the day, the queue to get in was shorter than usual. The cobblestone courtyard lay before us and, as we crossed the large open space between the wings, it felt like something was flooding into me, rising and falling and rising again. I was experiencing the

structure around us so intensely, its hundreds of thousands of granite blocks, its engulfing stillness and solidity,
compared to the mood that reigned in the rest of the city,
where everything was in constant motion, carrying with
it so many possibilities and promises. From what I could
remember I'd never thought of the Louvre as a historical place before, but knowing it had once been François
I's home, one of the homes he'd used outside Amboise,
made me see it in a new light.

We rode the escalator down to the museum entrance and
I took my daughter's hand as we went inside. We followed
the signs and the arrows – a shortcut signposted for everyone
who was there just to look at a single piece of art.

For a few years now, it had been said that Claude Monet's
Impression, Sunrise and Michelangelo's *The Creation of Adam*
had superseded the Mona Lisa in the competition for the
world's most famous painting, but you couldn't tell inside
the museum. There, the usual flocks of tourists were crowd-
ing the cool marble room where the picture hung, and as
usual the visitors seemed surprisingly moved by it. Either
this, or they were frantically taking pictures or talking about
how small it was or how silly it was that this was the picture you simply had to see when visiting one of the world's
greatest art museums.

It was further than I remembered between the Italian and
French Renaissance painting collections, and when I saw the

museum guards cordoning off the way to the other wings, I realised I wasn't going to get to see the portrait of François I after all.

Previously, I probably wouldn't have let my work, or even my desires, take a backseat to my daughter's but, as we stood next to each other in front of the painting, it surprised me that my own plans being dashed didn't matter so much, because the important thing was that she had been able to see what she wanted to see.

She gave me a bewildered smile. 'It's not *that* small,' she said. 'I thought it was going to be much tinier, because everyone always talks about how small it is.'

I nodded and looked at the painting, and back at her. I couldn't help but contemplate the distance and closeness between us, which must exist between parent and child, and I wished to always be accessible to her, and to her brother and sister. It was all I wanted, I realised, as this brand new thought rose up before me like a strange mountain. I put my arm around her shoulders and squeezed her close, and she leaned forwards and laughed out loud as we walked out of the room and through the galleries.

When I was around her age and taking frequent trips to Paris, I'd visited the Louvre often. I'd spend whole days sitting on the steps and by the windows in the sculpture hall, writing in my notebook and trying to draw the sculptures and statues: *Sleeping Hermaphroditus* or *Psyche Revived*

by *Cupid's Kiss*. As we were leaving the museum, I caught
sight of the courtyard from the other direction: the glass
pyramid and the clear blue sky opening up above it, and
it dawned on me that what I'd felt here as a young person
must have been security. Or was I making this up now,
because I felt so at home?

It was entirely possible that the king had hosted his
good friend Jean-François de la Rocque de Roberval in this
place, and perhaps her, too. Maybe she'd been here. If she
had visited Paris, it's not out of the question that this is
where she would have been. She could have ridden here
with Roberval and spent the night, maybe even lived here
for a spell. It was hard to grasp, but as we made our way
to Rue de Rivoli through the colonnade, the vaulted ceiling of which was as dark overhead as the cobbles were
underfoot, my head spun with the thought of her perhaps
having walked this same path.

We emerged on the pavement and were struck by the heat. The sun blinded us, reflecting off shop windows, flashing on the buildings' ornamentation and the golden tips of the park's black gates. We crossed the street to get to a nearby place where I remember once having dinner with a man who was more than twice my age. I hadn't actually wanted to have dinner with him, but he'd furnished me with so much writing material that I hadn't felt able to refuse his invitation.

My daughter found a seat on the large outdoor patio where all the chairs were facing in one direction and took her phone out of her pocket. I ordered us coffee and water and left for the bathroom. As I was passing through the restaurant, my skin prickled with unease when I caught sight of the tables at the back. That was where I had sat on that night so many years ago. I could recall him to a T: his glossy black hair and the dark, canine gaze that never once strayed from me. I suppressed the memory.

In the washroom outside the toilets I avoided my gaze in the mirror. I soaped my hands, rinsed and dried them and applied a matte red lipstick, which I knew my daughter liked, blotted my lips on a paper towel and tossed it away.

Back on the patio I saw the waitress leaning over our table, helping my daughter type the Wi-Fi password into her phone. I sat down and my daughter said she was just going to check Snapchat. She wanted to know what everyone else was up to right now, she said. I stifled an impulse to sigh – *But you're here now, why do you have to know?* – and took out my own phone and googled the portrait of François I. I looked at his large white nose and the pale hands he was holding out in front of him, his fingers elegantly folded over each other, like a true thinker.

François I is the man who is considered to be the creator of modern France. His ambition was to be a humanist regent and this is how he has been remembered. He is often described as a great patron of the arts, as a *protecteur des Arts et des Lettres*, a protector of art and the written word, which at first didn't fit with the picture I had of him as a tyrant – as if a tyrant couldn't also be keen on literature and modernity. It was he who laid the groundwork for the libraries and museums of France. Because it fell to the king to supply and administer justice in conflicts between members of the aristocracy, what happened to her should have come to his attention, but nothing in the public archives suggests it did. So either François had never found out what Jean-François de la Rocque de Roberval had done to the young relation he'd been given custody of – perhaps the whole story was covered up to protect Roberval, or to protect her – or he was privy to every detail and didn't see a problem with it.

I set my phone on the table and looked at my daughter. She was concentrating, typing and taking pictures of herself, making faces. Then she laughed loudly at whatever had popped up on the screen in her hand. I took my sunglasses out of my bag, wiped them with a napkin from the aluminium box next to the ashtray on the table and put them on.

I warmed my face in the sun for a moment before picking up my phone again. The unease that the memory of the dinner here years before had called up lingered in me. I remember having felt it then, a creeping through my body, a bass note resonating inside me throughout the dinner and our rendezvous, from when we first met and first spoke, when he came over and invited me to a private viewing at his gallery. Now that the feeling had returned, the disgust came back much more strongly, since I no longer had reason to force myself to disregard it.

I closed the webpage with Clouet's portrait of François I and visited one with his sister Marguerite de Navarre. This portrait is hanging in a museum in Liverpool and resembles that of her brother in the sense that they're both sitting in front of a red tapestry – though not the same one – and are both turned slightly to the side, regarding the viewer with a veiled gaze. The two of them are turning towards something else, something out of frame.

Marguerite de Navarre was often portrayed looking down and to the side, or with her gaze fixed in the distance as though in observation or contemplation. She gazes as she herself is being regarded. In Clouet's painting, unusually enough, she's looking almost directly at the viewer but is wearing the same introverted half-smile as Mona Lisa in *La Joconde*, something which led to this portrait long being considered the work of Leonardo da Vinci. The head scarf she's wearing is decorated with long rows of ox-eye daisies, called *marguerites* in French, which I took to be her flower. Naturally. By her hand sits a green parakeet, which is often thought of as a symbol of her renowned eloquence but is also assumed to stand for love and, because of its colour, passion – either because the painting was made in conjunction with her marriage to Henri de Navarre and her becoming queen, or simply because love was a recurring theme in her writing. I choose to believe the latter. Or rather, I choose to believe she had a reason for agreeing to be immortalised with the green bird, even though she didn't love Henri.

I took out a cigarette, lit it and inhaled the smoke, and when the waitress came to take an order from another table I caught my reflection in the glass panel in the door she opened. I wasn't the same person I had been the last time I'd been here. I was an adult now, and I had a life. A fantastic one, in fact. Such thoughts were soothing and the discomfort vanished. I no longer needed to subject myself to danger and threat to be able to write, to have something to write about. There was already so much around me, everything going on was more than enough. There was so much I couldn't understand and had no control over.

The reason I'd thought I needed the danger then related to my idea of what life was and what was worth writing about: what, up until that point, I had been taught was important. The man had radiated a confident, borderline hostile, masculinity that roused my disgust but was nonetheless irresistible. There was something vain and challenging about him; his pomposity, his erotic obstinance and the prejudices he expressed to me. It repulsed me, but it also came with a whiff of victory because these were the very behaviours I wanted to see and write about.

What didn't matter as much to me then was how I'd vacate myself in those situations, watching from outside my body and what I said; how I touched my hair and set my lips as I sat in silence, his eyes on me. It didn't make me ill at ease then. It was a part of the hunt; as if I were setting traps in a forest, waiting, then watching, then delighting in him stepping into each and every one.

To lure him in, I had to sacrifice part of my own security, if I did indeed want to write about how men behaved towards women, and how people behaved towards each other. If

anyone had suggested that this came at a price, I'd have dis-
missed it as an expression of a stereotype of women being
either sacrosant or prey.

I was noticing that I didn't feel this way anymore. I could
no longer dismiss my feelings as easily, dismiss their physical
effect on me.

My coffee was still so hot that the cup burned my fingers. I had to set it down and blow on it. My daughter had
disappeared inside her phone and I stubbed out the half-
smoked cigarette and allowed myself to vanish in mine. I
stretched my legs out on the pavement, leaned back and
returned to François I.

Having inherited a predilection for Italian Renaissance art
from his mother, he had cared for Leonardo da Vinci towards
the end of his life and let him live in a lesser castle in Amboise
that was connected to the larger one by a subterranean tun-
nel. This is how the Mona Lisa came into French possession,
the text said, and was why she was hanging in Paris. I read the
piece again and realised that I had actually spotted this in the
gallery – his place of death next to the name on the sign by
the painting: *Amboise*. I'd seen it, but hadn't given it a second
thought.

When the weekend was over and it was time to visit Roberval, the receptionist at our hotel explained that it was impossible to get there by taxi. It would be far too expensive, she said. I felt embarrassed when I told her that didn't matter. I could pay. I was on a business trip, I said, by way of excuse, and the village was practically on the way to the airport. In the right direction, at least. But she shook her head again.

'No, madame. It's absolutely impossible, madame.'

Ten minutes later I was sitting in the back seat of an Uber Black with my daughter by my side. In between us, the console was folded down and filled with bottles of Evian. It was cool and pleasant in the car, but I was uncomfortable and nervous. I was plagued by a familiar worry that settles in at the end of a trip, a sense of having spent too much money, and the disappointment of having to go home. It was clearly a result of conditioning. As a young person I'd so often found myself en route to the airport, leaving Paris even though I didn't want to. Not to mention the fact that I wasn't exactly sure where we were going. Nor could I remember where

I'd seen the chateau's address; I'd searched the Uber app and Google Maps to no avail.

We drove past Place Édith Piaf and towards the outskirts of the city, where it ends most abruptly and the network of roads is at its most complex. By the exit of the ring road and the country roads a recent accident ground everything to a halt. Our driver, Aymen, a man in a suit who I thought was my age but was most likely over a decade younger, took out his phone and called the taxi office to inquire about the address. When I heard that he wasn't getting any clarity, I felt even worse. Had I imagined that Château de Roberval still existed? Had I misinterpreted something I'd read? Then I remembered the chateau's Wikipedia entry. I opened the image folder in my phone and scrolled until I found the screenshot of the article. In the info box, the coordinates were plain and clear. I recited them for Aymen, who smiled at me in the rear-view mirror.

'No need to worry, madame,' he said and typed the numbers into his GPS. 'We'll find it now.'

I thought about the working conditions for Uber drivers and the polite distance they usually kept, like an invisible wall, and the dark suits and water bottles and the way they held the door open for you. It all seemed designed to create the image of luxury, as though you were being driven around by a private chauffeur rather than in a taxi. I had nothing against it; it was a welcome relief to skip the small talk and the looks from the driver. I wondered, though, if what I thought to be a pleasing discretion was a strategic decision, knowing that the driver would be rated – something the app encourages you to do. On the other hand, the driver could also rate the passenger: my own rating had dropped from 4.8 to 4.7 stars, I'd only noticed now. But Aymen was different. Not that he was intrusive or even spoke to us as he drove, but he radiated something rare that I recognised and that couldn't be ignored. Joy. He genuinely seemed to think this was fun.

The traffic eased. We pulled away from the city and onto the motorway and my daughter leaned back and said she was going to take this time to listen to a podcast she'd downloaded. I looked out of the window and saw how the countryside took over almost at once: acres of yellow and green passed by, flowering rapeseed and tall stalks of corn swaying in the hot breeze. In the fields white silage bales were scattered like giant gleaming marshmallows and we drove past medieval villages, their low, chalky stone walls and fountains so entrancing it made me ache. It was their sudden appearance, so close to the cars and road, and the way the afternoon sun gleamed in the dust around them.

We'd arranged for Aymen to wait while we visited the tower and the wall, and then I'd requested another ride via the app so he could drive us to Beauvais and its budget airport. I sat in silence, looking out of the window. All around the landscape repeated itself: the same wide fields and white villages, and it was like we were driving in circles, up and down the A1, on through uncommonly vivid wheat fields garnished by fluffy green thickets. Next to me on the seat was a paperback I was planning to read on the plane, an essay by an American journalist, the title of which had unsettled my daughter: *Why I Am Not a Feminist: A Feminist Manifesto*. Her reaction to it had made me cross and I said that maybe I should stick disclaimers on my books before showing them to her. This was also what was vexing me: I regretted the irritation I had displayed towards her. For several years now our conversations had revolved around identity and identity politics in various forms. I'd enjoyed partaking in her thoughts and had been happy to see that theories I'd engaged with years before, then seen as out of touch and irrelevant, now seemed to have 'spread' in exactly the way it had been said they never would. But for a while I'd been thinking that she was mainly parroting what she'd read and seen in her social media feeds, where the language seemed standardised and the world that emerged through it so spelled out, so devoid of complexity and nuance – almost as though an individual point of view was forbidden or as if art and literature had become impossibilities, as if her generation could take nothing on board unless they were already aware of its precise political implications. It was regrettable, but most of all I fretted over not being able to stop myself from taking my frustrations out on her. She was only a child

and I hadn't done much to invite her into my own thought
processes, and yet I expected her to understand them – as
though I hadn't really understood that we weren't one and
the same, but rather two separate people.

She took out one of her earbuds and spun it around her
finger. So this must be what was breaking them: unusable
earbuds littered our apartment. She began spinning it in the
other direction. 'Did you know you were going to have a girl
when you were pregnant with me?' she asked.

'No,' I said. I had an idea of where this was going.

'But did you know what you wanted to have?'

'Yes. I really wanted you to be a girl.'

She nodded and looked at me.

As I recalled, I hadn't dared find out the baby's sex when
I was expecting, because I feared some sort of negative con-
sequence. I really wanted a girl, like most people I knew –
men as well as women – but I suspected that there were
probably limits to the wishes one could have for a child,
and the midwives I met during my pregnancy seemed to
confirm my misgivings. You could wish for a child, for it to
be born healthy and to survive, but you couldn't specify its
gender and, just because you could find out a child's sex,
didn't mean you should.

I had never mentioned how much I wanted to have a
daughter the first time I had a child. Not to her and not to
anyone else. When she was little I tried to bring her up in

a gender-neutral way, even if I understood that probably wasn't possible (if nothing else, how could you know, really, that you were?), and now that she was older, I'd started to notice this tendency again. I wanted to downplay the importance of gender in our discussions, and I constantly tried to take gender out of our conversations because, in my experience, she always did the opposite.

The asphalt seemed newly poured but the road ahead looked uneven; the centre line was a rolling wave. I convinced myself that what I was feeling was normal parental guilt. Aymen, his expression still upbeat, glanced at me in the rear-view mirror. My daughter had gone back to her podcast, but after a while, she took out one earbud and handed it to me. Two people were talking about a new book neither of them had read and which they weren't planning on reading either because they'd seen on Twitter that it contained a word they felt should not be used. Not ever. They were furious at the author – all of his books should be boycotted; even the old ones were ruined by this mistake. I anticipated them changing the topic, but they wouldn't let it go, their voices and displays of emotion rising. It was so familiar. I had been similarly judgemental and poured out all my rage and sorrow in doing so, but now I was having difficulty breathing as I listened to them and remembered how the political discourse I'd partaken in seemed to focus solely on the individual.

My daughter noticed my displeasure.

'But do you, as a white woman, feel that you're allowed to write about whatever you like?' she asked.

'I don't know what I *feel*.' I sighed. 'In principle, I *feel* that anyone is allowed to write about anything. It's sort of the whole point, or one of the points at least, that we should be able to put ourselves in another person's ... It's ... I mean . . .'

My cheeks burned and I shook my head to dispel the irritation. She calmly raised her eyebrows and waited for me to finish my sentence, but I didn't. She took back the earbud and looked at me as if for my permission to keep listening on her own; I nodded, and she put the earbud back in and turned away from me. I looked past her, out of her window at the ever-unfolding landscape; I looked at her hair and the nape of her neck, and then at the thin white cord of the earphones running along her body and over the seatbelt. The silence made me feel mute inside, a testament to how unworthy I was of her attention; and this may have been the moment I saw her clearly.

I'd been viewing her as a representative of a generation and a problem, but in truth she was my child and she had turned to me. Her engagement was a bond between us, a way for her to connect to her origins. To me.

Thinking about it now, I wonder if she was trying to connect in other ways I hadn't noticed. I wonder if there have been others who tried too.

I checked the time on my phone. The road was clear, but it felt like we'd never get there. As though this thought struck the three of us simultaneously, Aymen took one hand off the wheel and opened the front seat storage compartment and fished out a handful of sweets in shiny paper wrappers, which he offered to us before eating one himself.

'Are you sisters?' he asked.

'No,' I said. I felt myself blushing, as much at the thought of the question being genuine as over the shame I felt because of it. I glanced up and caught him looking at me in the rear-view mirror again.

'You never know, right?' he said. 'You do look very much alike.'

He looked at my daughter and then at me and back at her.

She'd gone still, stiffened. 'Mum,' she said. 'Did he just ask if I was your sister?'

'Only because I'm wearing a baseball cap,' I said. 'You can't tell how old I am.'

'Or how young I am.'

'Right.'

We sat in silence.

Aymen's eyes were back on the road. He slowed down, signalled and turned into a roundabout and then onto another country road that looked exactly like the previous one. He accelerated. I watched the speedometer slowly move up the dial and sensed the speed, the pressure of my back on the seat behind me. Shortly thereafter the sign for Roberval appeared. Aymen gave a short whoop. His smile turned into a low, giddy laugh and he seemed to be enjoying the speed and the view, the car's forward momentum and the summer day we were driving through.

When I'd tried to imagine how it would be, I'd pictured myself walking down a narrow road, the last stretch before the chateau, making my destination clear to everyone who saw me. But when we arrived, there it was, right next to us, just like the medieval villages we'd driven by. There was no more than a half metre between the road and the castle wall – cars were zipping right past it. I pictured people in the cars on their way to airports or to the vet's or to work. There was no one there to see me. The village was empty.

Aymen pulled onto the gravel pitch in front of the chateau and parked in the shade of a chestnut tree. I unfastened my seatbelt and got out of the car. There wasn't a soul around – it was silent and hot. The sun was blazing. Between the gravel pitch and the castle wall ran a small paved road and a narrow pavement, and spread out in front of the wall was a lush lawn, almost unnaturally green and dense. Was anything more contemporary than a lawn like that? Across the road was an open square I'd seen on Google Maps. At home in bed, or at our kitchen table, I'd looked at it often. There was a dusty saturation to the photo, a listlessness not present in real life. It was hardly a square as you'd imagine one, but it wasn't just a turning area either. It had a name, Place du Château, and there was a parking lot, a brasserie that looked shuttered, a crooked telephone box and a by-road that led to some houses with small, square gardens. Where we'd driven in with the car was a village office and a street with some larger chain shops contained in buildings that matched the old architecture. The lane in front of the castle wall led to a few buildings that appeared to be as old as the chateau and very well preserved. I remember thinking that the people who lived there might be in receipt of some sort of funding for maintenance. Behind one of the buildings, a basketball net was mounted, and further on was one more building. That was it.

I started walking towards the tower alone. I'd expected it to feel a little threatening, and it did; I suppose I was thinking of him. On closer inspection, I was simply struck by its beauty. It probably hadn't occurred to me that the tower might be beautiful. I felt enraptured as I thought about actually being there now, and that she had almost certainly been there as well. It felt as though the tower were offering itself up to me, but when I got closer, the feeling vanished as quickly as it had arisen.

I was thinking about his sex as I was standing there. The image was so deeply banal, and yet it caught me off guard. I reached for the structure and touched the wall first, then the tower. The tower was probably a bit shorter than I'd expected but still tall enough to make it hard to discern the four sculpted faces atop the octagonal slate roof. I stood on my tiptoes, tilted my head and stretched upwards. The afternoon light was bright and I noticed I was squinting in an attempt to sharpen my gaze.

Aymen and my daughter stayed close to the car, each on their own side of it, clearly wondering what I was up to and what they were supposed to do with themselves while waiting for me. They wandered around, not saying anything, and when I turned back to the tower, it seemed to have taken on the sheen of the ordinary, which the wells and buildings we'd driven past also had; the ordinariness that sprung up around a sensational object if you got this close.

To think of all that this place holds.

When they arrive, they're surprised to be greeted by the old woman. *Damienne*. This was her name. She was the one who André Thevet would come to call an old bag but also a bawd and a procuress, as though she were responsible for it all, as though it were her fault or even her intention that it ended up the way it did. And even though he'd stated her name more than once in both *La Cosmographie Universelle* and *Le Grand Insulaire et Pilotage d'André Thevet*, others would refer to her otherwise. For example, James Phinney Baxter in *A Memoir of Jacques Cartier* from 1906 consistently calls her Bastienne instead of Damienne when he brings up this story. He must have thought it didn't matter.

Damienne heard them coming and stopped outside the pale archway, on her way to the castle's kitchen. She is hunched and clutching a goose. Its limp neck is draped over her hand and its head is hanging straight down, dark, its black beak pointing to the ground. According to Thevet, Damienne was sixty years old and hailed from Normandy, and considering what Marguerite would later tell him about how these events would unfold, this detail was perhaps deci-sive: for a long time, the region had lain outside France.

He wrote nothing about when Damienne entered the picture. Did Jean-François de la Rocque de Roberval enlist her so that he could have his young lady live with him at his castle, or was it that the young lady and the old servant were well acquainted, that Damienne was part of the household goods that came from her parental home, and was on one of the horses with them as they rode through the country?

I had given a lot of though to this point because it would have shaped how she experienced what would later happen to both her and Damienne – which was also my reason for visiting the tower.

Three contemporary records from the 1500s are proof of Marguerite's existence and the events that are today often associated with her name having taken place. Each recounts her story in its own way. They were all published many years after the fact, during the latter part of the century (imagining how long it must have taken to put a book out back then amused me).

According to the National Library of France, all three works were available to read online. I had my concerns about literature being digitised, but when it came to these old books, which I myself needed to read, I could only be pleased. How convenient that everything seemed to be available. The works had been scanned in full, flyleafs and all, and could be downloaded in various formats. I longed to bury myself in them, immerse myself in the text and forget everything else, everything about the time I was living in that was making me feel alienated and confused. I felt so old, even though I was barely middle-aged. I had such difficulty concentrating, and this wasn't limited to writing: I had discovered that I also had difficulties reading, which I hadn't been able to admit to myself because this felt even worse than finding writing challenging. Writing is always hard. My work on Marguerite, since it had become real work, largely comprised reading. It was a task I had imposed on myself: seeking out those three old books and trying to understand them, or at least understand some of them through sentences and fragments written by people who likely had first-hand information, to find out more about what had happened to her and to try to hear her words through theirs.

All three authors were prominent figures in France and Europe during her life, and at least two of them had met her. They certainly could have answered several of my questions, but in these books the answers were hidden in rewritings, fictionalisations and omissions of central facts. There were silences, omissions and lies, romanticisation and literary conceits. They each had their own motives for why they had chosen to tell her story at all, and for how they told it. Their own fears and urges permeated these works. In this respect, we were no different, and I was trying to remind myself that all of this was contributing to the sorrow I felt because, however I read them, I was merely scratching at the surface and forever at risk of missing something essential. These books had been written almost 500 years before I was born and were in a language I could barely command in its modern form. Their archaic nature was yet another veil of fog surrounding the story.

The source that seemed most compelling when I started this project was Thevet's great cartographical work *La Cosmographie Universelle*. Thevet was a royal cartographer, a good friend of Jean-François de la Rocque de Roberval, along with the royal siblings and many of their friends native to Angoulême in southern France where he'd joined the Franciscans, which he'd chosen to leave in favour of devoting himself to science. He is remembered as one of the Age of Exploration's great explorers, but for many years he did not travel to the countries he was writing about, relying wholly on first-hand accounts by others, like the one she had furnished him with during the interview that, he wrote, he conducted with her shortly after it was all over.

In *La Cosmographie Universelle*, the interview lays the foundation for a long and detailed account that has been considered highly credible since it is consistent with the content of other documents and with the work of geographer Richard Hakluyt, and even points to a number of specific statements that can only have come from her and which he could hardly have had any interest in fabricating.

Because André Thevet was Jean-François de la Rocque de Roberval's friend and Roberval was an influential person, he had nothing to gain by fabricating or exaggerating a story of this kind. On the contrary, he'd probably have considered how Roberval is presented, embellishing parts, toning down his wickedness. Because this is what I was wondering, as one seems to wonder when contemplating what befalls women because they are women: can it really have been that bad? Is it really as serious as it seems? And: haven't we talked about this enough yet? I was forever wondering. But then I felt a certain calm when I realised that none of this was likely to have been the least bit exaggerated, and I wasn't contributing to carrying on a baseless grumble throughout the centuries. No, the reality of the situation had probably been much worse.

La Cosmographie Universelle was published when André Thevet was approaching sixty, but when he wrote the part about her, he was in his thirties. I didn't know and hadn't seen anyone comment as to what extent the delay played into the complicated nature of the thing, such as his relationship with Jean-François de la Rocque de Roberval. I simply assumed that writing thousands of pages about the world must have taken time.

The second source was the king's sister, who was then one of the world's most powerful women. She had many names: Marguerite de Navarre, Marguerite d'Angoulême, Margot de Valois and, in addition to being a French princess, Queen of Navarre and Duchess of Berry and Alençon. She bore a prince's title otherwise reserved for men – she was a *prince capétien*. The first time I read about Marguerite de Navarre was in a book with brief entries about 'women who had changed the world' – something like that – a gift from a library in which I'd done a reading. I knew her name from Paris, from one of the exits at the Les Halles metro station. A small square is also named after her: it lies just beyond the top of the escalators leading out of the metro and on it now sits a large Lego shop. *Femme de lettres* it reads under her name on the street sign.

Marguerite de Navarre had studied Latin, theology and philosophy, Hebrew, Italian, German and Spanish, and continued to educate herself throughout her life. She fought with her brother in the Italian campaigns and rescued him when he was imprisoned after the Battle of Pavia. She came to be one of the French Renaissance's protagonists and played a crucial role in the Reformation's development in Europe. She is described as a gracious queen who devoted herself widely to social work and moved among the people in cities and villages without guards or other escorts. She established a care home for unmarried pregnant women and a special hospital for orphans in Paris, L'Hôpital des Enfants-Rouge, which had been on Rue de Bretagne, not one hundred metres from the bistro we visited upon arrival. This, I thought, was quite remarkable, like so much else about this project. All that seemed to come to light when I least expected it.

Because Marguerite de Navarre had honoured her duty to be at her brother's side, she spent much time in a sedan chair (so that's how you travelled back then!), en route between some of the many glorious castles he had built in France, and it is said that it was then that she wrote letters, poems, plays, pamphlets and short stories. I didn't know much about the development of the short story in Europe in the 1500s and at first the descriptions of Marguerite de Navarre's body of work didn't inspire me to read her. Nothing in her extensive output seemed to be worth it. To this day it happens that she is described as an amateur and as insignificant alongside the period's true literary greats, such as Rabelais or Montaigne: a queen who dabbled with her quill for lack of other diversions. In the assessments of her writings it's as though her status itself makes her a lesser author. I had read that she was dull, a weak stylist and sloppy, and that the short stories in her most famous work *The Heptameron* – or *L'Heptaméron des Nouvelles de très illustre et très excellente princesse Marguerite de Valois, royne de Navarre*, as it is written in the royal sigil in the scanned edition that I had long been using – were romantic historiettes. This didn't exactly entice me into reading them; I thought I'd let that be that and satisfy myself with the one that contains her interpretation of this story, the sixty-seventh story in the collection, entitled 'Nou. 67: Extreme Amour, & Austerité de Femme, en Terre Estrange' or, as it is called in the 1954 Swedish translation I'd recently got hold of: 'The Sixty-seventh Story.'

Standing in front of the tower, taking it in, I heard a car pull up and park in a free space by the road. Unease moved through me. If anyone asked what we were doing here, what would I say? Dust billowed around the car. A man and two boys with schoolbags got out and went into the house closest to the brasserie. When they caught sight of us I could tell they were checking us out, and I heard them speaking to each other. I turned back around.

The lawn was so strangely soft beneath my feet; above me foliage unfurled, green leaves reaching in every direction. The tree was higher and larger than the chestnut we'd parked under. The thick trunk was grey, the sharp curve in its middle familiar. It made me think of a tree I'd been writing about in a novel I'd abandoned to keep working on this. But why had I done that? I wasn't quite sure. I knew it was because I wanted to keep researching her in anticipation of the film script being commissioned, so I'd be prepared – but it was also because I was having trouble getting back into the novel. It had shut its doors on me.

What about her was so absolute that it thwarted every-thing else?

I'd long been saying that I wasn't going to write a book about this; I'd delighted in having a subject that for once had a given form. I'd convinced myself that it could only take one form, but this was no longer the case. What a pity, somehow, that everything always turned into a book, and there was nothing I could do to stop it.

The main reason I'd been trying to avoid writing the book was perhaps because a friend had asked me not to. She didn't think the story belonged to me – it belonged to her because she was the one who'd told me about it, and she wanted to keep it for herself. This knowledge was like a dull rumble that would rise through the text and rouse my fear and shame, but which also clarified my own position to me. It became ever more apparent that her feelings couldn't stop me.

However I tried to prevent it, the lone woman on the island found her way into everything I wrote and everything I did and this was also how my life worked. It was a like a machine. Everything was poured into and shaped by the writing, only to come back out through it again. I consumed everything that crossed my path.

It didn't occur to me then that others might not have allowed themselves to be embarrassed by this fact, and instead would have felt pleased that this was the way it was – that they were using their material and felt secure about the implications of their writing.

Beyond the tree was an opening in the wall, which was filled by a tall white-painted iron gate. Next to the gate was a small mailbox mounted on a post. Through the gate I glimpsed white garden furniture and, right in front of the castle, a bed of large, pale pink flowers reminiscent of hydrangeas, but which were probably some sort of peony. Peony poppies, maybe. It was hard to tell from this distance. Aside from the garden furniture, the flowers and some gauzy white curtains in a couple of the windows, there was no trace of a human presence, but the wide-open gate could very well mean that someone had recently driven away in a car or was soon to return. Upon closer inspection I saw that the window in the castle door and several on the bottom floor were boarded up from the inside with what looked like large wooden planks.

Though this didn't necessarily mean no one was home, it put me at ease. I didn't want any contact with the people who owned the castle or who lived there, if anyone did. I didn't want anyone to emerge and ask what I was doing. I didn't want to talk about what I was doing, not with the people who were connected to Jean-François de la Rocque de Roberval, even if it was only through their ownership of what had once been his property, nor with anyone else. Once I would have wanted this: I'd have wanted to let anyone who'd crossed my path into the text and into my life to see what they would do with it – and how I could shape their actions – but now I wanted to shut out as much as possible. I didn't want anything more than what was already there to find its way in. There was so much already. It was almost impossible to keep it all out of the way.

In my bag was a notebook that I'd picked up for the first time in a long time that morning. I'd started by writing a few sentences on one page and had ended up filling several pages, but the book was otherwise empty, except for a spread at the back on which the children had drawn, probably when we were out somewhere and I'd needed to work so had asked them not to bother me. I still bought notebooks when I found the ones I liked: compact booklets with thick black covers and labels on the front, which were available at a stationery shop in Berlin. The woman who worked there would point out that I could buy them online, but I never did, and in recent years I'd stopped writing in them entirely.

A notebook is security for a person who writes – like keeping tampons in your bag. Note-taking in this way is a kind of writing you can do anywhere, but I'd stopped enjoying doing it, and being at the tower reminded me why this was. It's the feeling of being somewhere, but not being able to experience it because you'd rather be writing about it; of never being fully present because your mind is always in the text, on your way to it or broken by the difficulties of trying to reach it. It had probably never been any different. This practice had been so fundamental to me that I'd hardly given it a second thought before, but I'd been sensing for a while that it was in the process of loosening up. In pace with the children growing up, a space had grown around me. I'd started to look at myself, look at all that writing had been to me, and was entertaining certain thoughts and sensations that I suspected spoke to another way of life. I thought I could find a different way of being and, standing between the tower and my daughter and Aymen at the car, I no longer felt entirely comfortable with the way my writing made it hard for me to grasp reality and participate in it.

When I thought about this, an echoing emptiness rang through me. I'd sensed it coming, but this didn't mean it scared me any less. Maybe it was the memory of the dinner with that man at the café near the Louvre that made me conceive of my writing in yet another way – after all, there were so many ways of looking at it because it impacted everything I felt and everything I was. Writing had driven me into a vulnerable existence, but it had also been a way for me to guard myself against what I thought was a threat to me. It had upheld my solitude, but also its accompanying challenges, and in turn what those challenges had led to.

I knew there were writers who were frightened by the thought of identifying their patterns, and I'd suspected that was because they didn't want to solve their inner mysteries, because then what would there be left to write about? But now it was clear to me that this wasn't what was at risk, at least not for me. My reluctance stemmed from the question of what would happen if I became a person who no longer needed to hide away or protect herself. What would happen to my writing if I no longer needed it for this function – who would I be then?

Writing had been a way of exploring what it was to be human, the life everyone else seemed to be participating in, without actually having to participate myself. Of not having to need other people and not having to be subject to the same relentless laws as everyone else, the laws of loss and vulnerability. But it had also been a way to not have to be a woman: to look, instead of being looked at. In this way I could, without repercussion and sometimes unseen, access certain spaces, physical or emotional spaces, spaces of experience – without really having to be there, or without subjecting myself to the status quo because my loyalty lay elsewhere.

Paris was a crowning example of one such space for me, but the village of Roberval with its 347 inhabitants was not. I had wanted to go there for the sake of the text; the text had not come to be because I wanted to go there. There were other reasons for its genesis, even though I wasn't yet quite clear what they were. At that time I also felt a remarkable disinterest in getting closer to Jean-François de la Rocque de Roberval, or rather a *reluctance*. He had built the tower, she

had been there (she must have been), and by going there I
found myself closer to him as well as to her. Their hands had
touched the stones I was touching, their feet had stood on
this ground. On the lawn? I couldn't help but doubt that it
was the same place it had been 500 years ago. If the coordinates, the tower, and the wall were the same, but everything
else had changed, could it be said that it was the same?

Time had transformed this place with buildings and roads,
the din of traffic had arrived but so had the trees and bushes,
every leaf and blade of grass. I took a few pictures of the
greenery behind the walls and was gripped by a desire to find
out what type of plants they were, to photograph each one I
saw, so that when I got home I could determine which plants
had been around back then, which ones she could have seen
and touched and smelled. Ivy climbed over the wall and up
the tower; between the stones grew stonecrop; and from the
mortar rose slender blood-red flowering stalks. I had never
doubted the durability of stone, but as I stood there taking
in the foliage twining itself around the stones I saw that the
flora, with its mutability, its capacity to adapt to whatever
came its way, was just as strong.

I'd been struck by a similar thought that morning in
Les Halles. There, in the middle of the city, so much had
been built since her lifetime: the majestic cathedrals and
monuments were still there, but between them time had
had its way. The medieval market had become a shopping

centre, which was undergoing another renovation, and what I wanted to see could barely be glimpsed beneath the architectural palimpsest of eras gone by. The place I was seeking was in these neighbourhoods, but that's all I'd established ahead of the trip and was probably why I was so surprised when it finally dawned on me as I was there. The realisation was still unsettling to think of now, hours later. It was an incredible, remarkable coincidence.

For the most part, I resist critical interpretations of a text based on the author's biography – possibly too much so. It's probably because I have a persisting suspicion that this type of interpretation affects women who write differently than it affects men, because what men write about is considered universal, whereas women ostensibly only write about themselves. (Because the cleft between writing and being a woman is still unbridgeable?) That said, I had read *The Heptameron* precisely because its tales are said to be based on true events. And the more I gathered about what Marguerite de Navarre's life had been like, the more her stories intrigued me. I wanted to see what she had made of her experiences, how she'd handled them as literature.

Marguerite de Navarre considered the story collection to be her life's work. It was her version of Giovanni Boccaccio's *Decameron*, with a framing story that she'd also borrowed from him in part: five men and five women, all literary versions of Marguerite de Navarre's friends and people in her circle, are on their way home after taking the waters in the Pyrénées but are delayed by a flood. They

seek shelter in the Notre-Dame de Serrance convent in
Béarn where they pass the time telling each other stories
and discussing morality.

What interested me most was what had become clearer
for Navarre's readers in the past century, namely the contra-
dictory assumptions about women addressed by so many of
these stories. In the preface to Tale LXVII, one of the men,
Simontault, comments:

> *Tis no new thing, ladies, to hear of some virtuous act on*
> *your part which, methinks, should not be hidden but rather*
> *written in letters of gold, that it may serve women as an*
> *example, and give men cause for admiration at seeing in the*
> *weaker sex that from which weakness is prone to shrink.*
> *I am prompted, therefore, to relate something that I heard*
> *from Captain Roberval and divers of his company.*

Aside from the book being a tribute to Giovanni Boccaccio,
The Heptameron is also said to have been a gift from Navarre
to her brother, a collection of stories to entertain him as he
lay ill with the fever that led to his death. In Cognac, south-
western France, where they grew up, Boccaccio was reified.
Navarre's intention had been to write one hundred stories,
as he had, following a theme that would play out over the
course of ten days one early autumn, but she didn't make it
past the seventy-second tale and the eighth day, before she

died in Paris on 21 December 1549. The book was published posthumously nine years later.

Now I think that Tale LVXII and its hidden message about what Marguerite de la Rocque had been subjected to should have been enough to get me to see the other stories in a different light, but it took me looking into more recent literary criticism which re-evaluated Marguerite de Navarre's work. Apparently I needed academic authorities to point out the obvious fact that she had been overlooked as a writer. Some days I'd asked myself if it was because I'd lost my ability to think critically, like I thought I'd lost my ability to think in general – could my brain have shrunk, as I'd read it could from stress? – and consequently I hadn't been able to see how her legacy as an author had been coloured by the fact that she was a woman writing about questions related to women's lives. More likely, however, was that I simply didn't *want* to get into it. I was no longer as inclined as I had once been to conduct a gendered reading; not because I doubted the relevance of one, but because of how this approach seemed to be misused by others. It was too sad.

Among the articles I'd found that highlighted the innovative and subversive aspects of Marguerite de Navarre's literary output was one by a researcher who said it was impossible to prove that she had written all seventy-two stories of *The Heptameron* herself. In the 1500s, an author

was more of an editor, a collector of stories whose under-
taking had less to do with originality than compiling, man-
aging and renewing what others had already written. On a
deeper level, it was probably not unlike an author's work
today – ideas about literary authenticity were different
then – so perhaps it didn't matter if some of the pieces
had been written by others. According to the article, this
applied to the last four stories.

I was devastated: I thought Tale LVXII was one of the
added ones.

I'd read the article late at night, in early autumn, and
I was probably tired or maybe something else had made
me bungle such simple arithmetic, but this new eventuality that emerged as a result of my mistake was shatter-
ing. It was one factor of uncertainty too many for me, not
to mention one that influenced fundamental elements of
how all of this had transpired. If Marguerite de Navarre
hadn't written the story about the woman on the island,
then who? And if she hadn't managed to write one hundred stories in her lifetime, why would the publisher have
chosen to add only four? If the stories had been added for
the book's publication, wouldn't the reasonable thing have
been to ensure there would be one hundred stories, as she
had wished? I went to bed and before I fell asleep I decided
to forget it all, to keep my own story intact, as I wanted it
to be.

The third contemporary source was François de Belleforest, a translator, author and poet who was an acquaintance of Marguerite de Navarre's and who also wrote short stories. Where her inspiration was Boccaccio, his was the Italian monk Matteo Bondelli, whose stories had taken their inspiration from the *fabliaux*, the most immoral metrical form in French medieval literature and one on which Shakespeare would later base some of his most famous dramas. François de Belleforest was significantly younger than the other two. He was born in 1530 in the region of Comminges in the Midi-Pyrénées in southern France, was orphaned and taken in by Marguerite de Navarre's court in Pau, where she was sheltering Calvin, Erasmus and Rabelais and hosting a salon called New Parnassus. Among the articles I found on the web about François de Belleforest none brought this up, but I drew the conclusion that it must have been there that he, who came from a poor soldier's family, discovered the Italian form of the novel that he would devote himself to and in which he would incorporate Marguerite de la Rocque's episode, in his *Histoires Tragiques* published in 1570.

And then there were Elizabeth Boyer's books. Boyer was a lawyer and a political scientist, born in 1913 in Ohio, died 2002, and reportedly a feminist. She had written a historical novel about Marguerite de la Rocque and another book that seemed to be the most comprehensive one ever published on the subject. *A Colony of One: The History of a Brave Woman*

was self-published in 1983, and as far as I could see, it contained extensive notes.

Searching for it online and in the library, at first I'd almost
felt relieved at how hard it seemed to get a copy of it. Impossible, even. It meant I wouldn't have to engage with another
person's ideas about the young woman who'd started to take
up a disproportionate amount of my time and who, as such,
I regarded as mine. As though I'd made her up.

But then an email arrived. I'd set up an alert for the title
on Amazon, and it was a message notifying me that a copy
had turned up: used from a seller in Wyoming, dust jacket
intact with a few minor tears in the bottom corner. It cost
almost 1,500 kronor (£125) excluding shipping. I knew I had
to order it right away because I might not be the only one
looking for it, but instead of clicking on the link I opened
my bank app and took care of some bills I'd put off for so
long that payment reminders had started turning up. When
that was done, I checked my email again and then went on
Instagram. There were a few accounts I enjoyed following,
and once I'd visited them, a few others appeared in my feed,
and I couldn't stop looking: there were celebrities filming
their children cooking oatmeal in their kitchens and young
women showing the books they liked as part of still-lifes with
teacups and flowers.

Then I went back to the email with the order link and
clicked on it.

Two weeks later, I received a text message with a dispatch note stating that the book could be picked up at my local delivery point. It had been raining non-stop all day, a cold rain, its icy chill presaging the weather that I knew was on its way. I went down to the tobacco shop where my book post was sent and where the employees sometimes seemed to give me pitying looks because of how much I had to carry home and read, and by the time I got back to the apartment I was drenched. I shook the rain off my coat and hung it up in the hall and then tore the tape off the package, the brown paper falling to the floor. I'd throw it away later.

The book was in much better shape than the description on the website had suggested. The dust jacket gleamed with a slightly sepia-toned photograph that spanned the front and back jackets, depicting a bedrock shore, which I took to be the island, and what lay beyond it, the archipelago. The title was centred in a large typeface. I wondered if Elizabeth Boyer started her own publishing house because no one else had wanted to publish the book, or because no one had wanted to publish it in this lavish format. I opened the book in the hall, touched the shiny paper which smelled of wax and something else so tangible and corporeal I thought I could sense everyone who'd held it before me, their palms and fingers. But presumably no one had leafed through it in ages. It had probably spent years on a shelf, as books can do when no one is thinking about them, until they become another detail of an interior, part of a pattern no one considers anymore.

On the back flap was a portrait of the author holding a canoe overhead against a backdrop of water and bedrock. She looked giddy, beaming with joy. She'd made it. She was on the island. I envied her a little, even though I wasn't sure if I wanted to make the trip myself. No roads led to the island, Boyer wrote. It could only be reached by boat or by bush plane, and even if communications had improved since she'd visited, such a trip would still be long – and I didn't want to be away from my husband and children more than I already was.

It was a new feeling, not wanting to leave them.

Still, when I could neither write nor step away from the computer, I'd find myself googling how long it would take to get there and how much it would cost. I wondered what it would be like to see the cave in person, how it would feel if I ever had the chance to climb up the mountain and seek it out – make my way in and lie down deep inside where she had lain.

I went through the image gallery at the end of the book, preceding the almost one hundred pages of notes that Boyer had so generously included, and soon I was faced with a picture of the exterior of the cave. The caption said it went by 'Margaret's Cave', a rock shelter with two openings, one to the south and one to the east, one larger and one smaller. It was hard to see how large the openings were because there was no person in the photo for scale. I kept flipping and found several pictures of Château de Roberval as well. They were credited to a different photographer, so it was possible that Elizabeth Boyer hadn't been there. Maybe she'd thought it was too long a journey? As far as I knew, she had no children, but there was a foundation named after her for single mothers in higher education and a feminist league for professional women who were against abortion, which she had founded in 1968. This last bit confounded me and I kept checking to be sure I hadn't misunderstood, but I didn't dig any deeper.

The photographs, mostly colour, were out of focus and faded. One was of Roberval almost exactly as I had seen it, but the difference was that the front door was ajar and the windows were hung with long white curtains. I wondered if the photographer had been inside and if she had spoken with the owners and what explanation she had offered for why she was taking the picture. Or could Boyer have bought the images from a photography agency? One of them showed the pale castle from the back, and when I looked closer, I saw water in the foreground. It said it was part of the old castle's moat, a moat that must have belonged to Jean-François de la Rocque de Roberval, a wide trench that surely had been dug to protect his forefathers and him. It felt strange. In all the time we'd spent there, it had never occurred to me

to walk around the castle and look at the back. Why hadn't
I done that?

I lingered in the hall with the heavy book in my hands. I
was tired from the rain and of autumn itself. My hair was still
wet, dripping from wisps onto the pages.

In addition to the photos from Roberval were some from
a few other French villages with possible connections to
her. Sermet, Sauveterre, Nontron. Sand-coloured buildings,
castle ruins, fountains. On one page was a simple drawing of
the route through the archipelago of what was once called
the Sainte Marthe islands, as plotted by Roberval's famous
navigator, Jean Alfonse de Saintonge; and on another was
a rendering of one of the ships Jacques Cartier sailed on his
voyage to the same region a number of years earlier. As I
was leafing through, I saw a chalk portrait of Marguerite
de Navarre with a lap dog on her knee, and the same study
of Jean-François de la Rocque de Roberval that I had seen
before, as well as handwriting and period documents, some
of which bore his signature.

In the midst of all of this I found the drawing, enlarged
on a full page of its own. I didn't understand what it was. I
stepped over the discarded packaging on the floor and went
further into the apartment, holding the large book out in
front of me. I set it on the kitchen table and switched on the
light to get a better look. What I saw on the page with the
illustration was a blackish-grey muddle of indecipherable

shapes and marks shooting off in all directions, scratches
and lines. I saw the palm tree, but didn't recognise it as such:
its sprawling shape stood out against the middle of the darkest area and made it look like everything else had sprung
from it. I couldn't make sense of the picture, but I stayed
with it. Something about it was powerful yet unsettling, evil
and sinister, and it seemed to be the reason the image was
impossible to descry.

I couldn't interpret the image but neither could I stop
looking at it. I dried my hair with a kitchen towel, got up,
made myself tea and sat back down, the teacup beside the
open book. When I reached for the cup, I happened to turn
the page and find a reprint of the drawing, smaller in size, a
facsimile of the entire spread in André Thevet's *La Cosmographie Universelle* for which it had originally been drawn.
Or for which I assumed it had been drawn, but how could
I know? She may have drawn it herself, for her own sake,
because she wanted to, or perhaps Damienne or the man
without a name had, or a third party who'd heard about
what had happened.

I CAN'T REMEMBER how long it took me to start reading *A
Colony of One*, but I remember putting it off because I worried I wouldn't be able to take in the essential information I knew it contained. I drew it out because I feared I

wouldn't be able to make anything of it. My expectations had grown so large. She had become such a big part of my inner life – but I still wasn't having particularly involved thoughts. Mostly they consisted of recurring images, which I wanted to preserve in their current form for a little while longer; I saw her on the island, the mountain. I saw the snow and the ice and the empty ocean, twigs and stones; her body climbing and running, limping after she stumbled at the bottom of a ravine, short of breath and arms waving as she raced down to the beach.

The book in her possession is the 1523 *Nouveau Testament* from Maison Simon de Colines in Paris. It's a leather-bound chignon Bible with red and gold plates. It is barely seven centimetres in height and is made to be hidden in a chignon; that's how she carries it on the ride to the chateau at Roberval and later when she boards the ship in the La Rochelle harbour.

I can just see her lifting her hand to touch it, hesitating, and only nudging her bun, one finger grazing the nape of her neck, the hand holding still.

Is the book already of great importance then or has it been foisted on her and she'll only gravitate towards it later? (Why do I think religion had to be foisted on her?) In her story in *The Heptameron*, Marguerite de Navarre wrote that she – 'the poor woman' as she calls her, and which made me cringe upon first reading – had always put her faith in God:

> . . . and since she found all her consolation in Him, she carried the New Testament with her for safety, nourishment and consolation, and in it read unceasingly.

When I embarked on this project, I probably couldn't have predicted how much of this would be about faith. Her being a Protestant is assumed to be a fact for the simple reason that he, Jean-François de la Rocque de Roberval, was. His name is on the long list of dissidents that was read aloud after the so-called Affair of the Placards in Paris, a number of years earlier, when anti-Catholic posters were plastered all over the city and even on François I's bedroom door.

On this occasion the king intervened and saved his friend from being hung and burned at the stake outside Notre-Dame along with other Reformation activists and, as I understand it, Jean-François de la Rocque de Roberval continued to, more or less, openly profess his new faith for the rest of his life, in spite of the persecutions that befell Protestants, which would only get worse in his lifetime.

This suggested a fidelity that didn't align with my impression of his character so far. I think I was overestimating the inherent evil in religion and in Christianity, but also the goodness I thought should accompany a strong belief in God. I thought Roberval was a hypocrite – he couldn't possibly have seen what he did to her as being in the service of God.

Later it became clear to me that this is probably exactly how he saw it.

I couldn't really trust my own assumptions when it came to the Divine or an individual's faith, because I didn't know much about it. I didn't know much about what God was or could be and what I once had known, I'd buried deep inside me. I grew up in an atheist home in a secular environment, I hadn't been baptised and wasn't a member of the Church of Sweden.

Elizabeth Boyer's main evidence for Marguerite's Protestantism was that she was brought up Protestant at a time when, among the French aristocracy, renouncing one's religion simply wasn't tolerated. As I read this I felt sorry for the people living then, in such strict times. I didn't take into account the fact that I had periodically believed in God and had felt impelled to keep this secret for fear of what others would think. Neither did I consider how I had made excuses for myself to the people around me when I decided to join the Church of Sweden.

It had happened the first winter I was a mother of three, when I crossed through the cemetery near our house twice each day. The church itself was built with stone and in a so-called Greek cross plan, with the bell tower in the centre and positioned so it could be seen from a distance, not only from the surrounding neighbourhoods but also from streets and squares in other parts of the town. It towered high on a hill between our street and the one the nursery was on, and I'd pass it on my way there and back with the two youngest in the pram, after dropping their sister off at school.

Thinking about it now, I don't recall the effort it took to leave my daughter at school in the mornings those first years, before she started walking herself. I must have had to squeeze the double pushchair through the school's narrow front door and park it inside, where it fit, just, and then pick up my youngest and leave her brother in the pushchair while I carried my younger daughter and held her sister's hand as I rushed up the old wide stairs to the third floor where the other children would throw themselves at us, shrieking, wanting to look at and say hi to the baby, before I'd run with her back down all those stairs, to comfort my son in case he'd started crying. Then I'd strap her in and wrangle the pushchair out of the door again.

It was supposed to be the lightest model of its kind; the so-called chassis was made of a special reinforced aluminium. The height of the handlebar was adjustable and, in addition to buying thick padded bunting bags to tuck the children into, we'd purchased winter wheels for the pushchair, which would roll smoothly even through slush and then mud, after the streets had been sanded and the slush had melted. Still, with the two children inside, it was very heavy: as soon as the slight incline before the church began, I had to push with all my might.

At the pre-school I would leave my son with the infant group. Then I would roll the pushchair out again, notic-ing the church's yellow bell tower as soon as I stepped into the lane and walked back, my eyes on the graves and the memorial grove. From whichever direction I approached, the church looked big, and when I came closer, it seemed even larger. It made me feel small, walking down the snowy gravel paths along the church walls, braced for the weather and with the giant, black pushchair in front of me.

On one side of the gravel path were the great poets – all men from what I could see – buried beneath towering ornamented stones. One of few women who had been laid to rest among the renowned was the foreign minister, who had been murdered one day on her way to buy a blouse in a department store. A square had also been named after her, an insignificant turning point on the city's outskirts. Below the cemetery's avenue was an area where dummies and teddy bears had been laid by the gravestones. A new cross had been erected there that winter. On it was a plastic folder of drawings that someone regularly changed, when the moisture and snow seeped under the plastic, wetting the paper and blurring the colourful chalk marks.

In addition to the gravestones the church was surrounded by dark trees and soft drifts of white snow, or maybe that's just how I picture it now – this place forever blanketed with snow in winter. As I approached it with the pushchair, I'd take everything in, how beautifully it all came together, and then my gaze drifted to the walls further afield, the charnel house with its ironwork and inscriptions, the avenue splitting the cemetery in two and dividing the resting places. Rows of maples, chestnuts and linden trees stretched their bare branches skywards and whenever I reached them I gazed at their dark trunks, the grooves in the blackening bark and how the lines ran alongside each other like crooked engravings.

On some days all I saw was the beauty of the church and its grounds, but on others it struck a chord I couldn't put into words but I knew was fundamental. It was like something in me was ending. Not that I'd thought I was immortal up until that point and that life would go on forever – I've never been one to think that way – but for reasons I couldn't or didn't want to see then and which have now become apparent, as things do after you turn forty, I'd persuaded myself that what drove other people didn't apply to me: I was a person who stood outside the cycle of birth and death that lays the foundation for human existence. Loss mattered nothing to me, neither did my continued existence matter.

I notice just how dramatic this seems now that I'm seeing it in writing, but up until that winter the notion had been like a plumb line in me. In any case, it had apparently dawned on me, at least to an extent, that this notion was not accurate, but as I made my daily trek with the pushchair past the house of God, I imagined that it was this place that was changing me, as though what radiated from the church building itself was relieving my burden, opening and emptying me.

I started taking my time crossing the burial ground on those mornings and afternoons and I noticed that the church came to mind more frequently, as well as other things to do with it, even when I wasn't nearby. A relative explained to me that churches have always had this effect on people; they were built for it, for instilling fear. And this may have been true. Walking there each morning made me fear God, fear him for what he might have in store for me.

For us.

I saw her on the desert island in that dark cavern and urged those places inside me to the fore. To be as alone and isolated as she was there. The images spoke to me, comforted me. How she, body heavy, moved across the mountain searching for another spring after the first had frozen over. Her hands clasped around a stone, breaking holes in the ice, sinking into the cold water below, pulling up long black threads of muck from the bottom. The view behind her, the whiteness, the endless expanse. But eventually something broader overtook my thoughts: this whole story, and how it had been told, what manner of thing it was.

The three contemporary sources often contradicted each other when it came to basic information, but when I laid them side by side I saw them as a fabric, threads woven into something seemingly greater than the sum of their parts – and what went unsaid also spoke to me. To read those old texts was to uncover a mystery within a mystery and soon my questions were no longer only about her or how they talked about her and why, but also about the sources themselves and their relationships to her, which roles they or the people who were close to them played in the story.

The obvious differences between these texts also reflected the breadth of what was written about her later; there seemed to be everything from academic works to journalistic accounts and literary depictions – novels such as Boyer's – that I would have rather not known anything about. I wasn't planning on reading them. The covers showed images of a beautiful woman, eyes on the horizon, long hair rippling in the wind – an aesthetic that for me was proof enough that those books, the ones that had already been written about her, were trifling and perhaps even ridiculous. But there was another image that came up when I googled her and which constituted a sort of threat in my eyes. It was a photograph of a woman with a gun and looked like it was from a film production. Each time I saw it, it made me wonder if someone might not have already made a TV series or movie about her.

I had found a number of works on Google Books that recounted and described the story as an untold story; a forgotten female fate lost to history as, it was agreed, female fates always ended up. Part of me wanted to see it this way too, but the more I read, the clearer it became that she was much discussed. It bothered me that many other authors, researcher and writers must have also heard her story and incorporated it into their work. Into their lives?

When I searched for François de Belleforest's novella, which had a long title that described the entire plot, I got lots of hits for the title of the book, but I couldn't find the novella itself. I typed in several words: *demoiselle*, *île*, *capitain*, and tried different letters to make the spelling more modern, but it didn't help. It was so strange. All the world's old tomes seemed to have been catalogued, by Google Books or by university libraries in various countries, and yet it was as if I couldn't find anything I needed – they'd either been checked out of the library already or the website I needed to visit was temporarily down.

I probably wouldn't have admitted it then, but the truth is that I kept bumping up against the thought that someone today was trying to embellish Jean-François de la Rocque de Roberval's legacy, and was going to pains to hide her history.

To continue hiding it.

I did what I could to bat such ideas away. They made me feel like a conspiracy theorist, like the Facebook 'friends' I either hadn't seen in years or didn't actually know who posted videos about how the earth was flat. (It was a world view that had initially interested me – when I thought it had been a belief widespread in the 1540s, and before it had become clear to me that even by then the theory had already been dispelled. I had been amused by the idea of writing about seafaring in an age when people thought it was possible to sail right over the edge of the world.)

After many ifs and buts I stumbled across an article that clarified that *Histoires Tragiques* was a mammoth work. It wasn't enough to find a book with that title by François de Belleforest: I would have to find the right volume – the third history in the fifth part, as it turned out. That's where his account was.

The search was also complicated, of course, by the fact that there were many books with the same title because *histoires tragiques* was also the name of a genre that François de Belleforest, and Marguerite de Navarre, worked in. The genre has been characterised as stories that address the darkest parts of mankind, the most heinous acts.

My French was nothing to reckon with anymore. I often felt ashamed when I attempted to speak it, either because I couldn't get a word out or because I could hear how infantile my utterances must have sounded. It was a mix of my old school French and street slang I'd learned as a teen, when I was travelling to Paris from Sweden as often as I could. Mine was a language that couldn't handle an adult conversation, much less a historical text.

I put great effort into trying to read the source material, and François de Belleforest was even more of a challenge than Marguerite de Navarre and André Thevet, not least because he had inserted a long cryptic song about her in the middle of the story. I could make out snatches of the verses and of the plot, but at the slightest hitch I'd get lost and start bouncing around the text. I looked up words I didn't understand and made associations with new ones, googled one thing, typed another into Google Translate.

It bothered me that I couldn't really see where the line was between my own limitations and the sources' attempts at covering certain things up. I still don't really know how it

turned out this way, but what I resisted most when I began
my research about her was surely the most obvious thing to
do: check Wikipedia. I think it had a lot to do with that pro-
tectionism, my dislike for the idea that anyone could visit the
site and read about her as easily as they could google pasta
recipes or descriptions of quarks or black holes or anything
else. Meanwhile, I was also like Simontault in *The Heptameron*: I wished for women's historical exploits to be remembered. Or did I?

One morning I'd woken up with a creeping sense of
unease that I took to be my subconscious telling me not to
drag this out any longer. I turned on the computer and in a
second was on the Wikipedia page about her. There it said
fl. 1536–44 after her name, Marguerite de la Rocque. *Fl.
Floruit.* Third person singular perfect of *florere*, to blossom.
She blossomed. Could what have happened to her during
those years be described as a blossoming? Had she been
alive now, and had some of what had befallen her then
befallen her now, it's possible she would have seen it that
way. It's ever-present, deep inside our stories: the idea
that the worst leads us forwards, and what doesn't kill us
makes us stronger, and that each and every one of us is a
hero overcoming challenges so that we can stand up in the
end and *tell our story*. Perhaps she also came around to this
view because this mindset was the same then. Or because
it was true.

The year 1536 was a familiar one. It appeared on a Canadian history website that was the second hit when I'd searched her name, what I presumed to be her full name. It said the same thing there as on Wikipedia, that she had been sworn in as *seigneureuse* for two regions, Languedoc and Périgord, on 17 November 1536, and it called up an imagined scene: a young woman surrounded by men in a dark chapel in Amboise who, during a feudal ceremony, is being made the owner of the land her father has left behind. The scene was as recogniseable as the one in the carriage had been: she is standing next to the men in the dark chancel, her face pale and soft compared to theirs, her hair combed back and gathered under a black headscarf fixed in place with a high diadem of the same colour. I saw her small white hands and her embroidered clothing, the men's gazes meeting above her head.

Her youth reinforced my image of how a young girl could be in possession of riches and still be defenceless, and I started thinking about how young she had actually been. How early could she have become one man's associate and fall in love with another, do everything else she had done? I had just been at the Guadalajara International Book Fair with my latest novel and during the reception at the ambassador's residence in Mexico City I'd been seated next to a woman who I immediately liked. She had such an engaged, clear way of speaking, while also sounding as if everything she was saying

was carefully considered. She told me she'd been hired for a
project that aimed to limit the number of teen pregnancies
in the country. When I asked her how old the girls were, she
smiled and said with obvious sarcasm that the words 'teen
pregnancies' weren't exactly accurate because most of the
girls had yet to enter their teens. Rather, they were between
nine and twelve years old. The men who'd been with them
were up to triple their age.

'You can imagine,' she added.

She stuck her fork into the poached salmon on the plate
in front of her, almost a perfect match in colour to the
T-shirt – THE FUTURE IS FEMALE it read – she was wearing under her blazer and, as she inspected her fish, she gave
voice to the questions I was about to ask, about how many
of the nine- to twelve-year-olds could be thought to have
acted of their own free will.

We couldn't know, but the closest we could come to
understanding was to ask ourselves what 'free will' might
mean in such a context.

But when it came to Marguerite, I wanted to know.

Her imagined thoughts appeared in my mind, just as the
thoughts of many others appear there all the time without my
questioning it – but when it came to sex, this didn't feel like
enough. The question of what she actually felt and thought
consumed me. I so dearly wanted to be sure of something in
all this. I think I wanted assurance, or at least a nod acknowl-

edging that what I was imagining about her was true. That it wasn't unreasonable to think that the catastrophe had taken flight inside her.

I imagined her desires and her fantasies, her will, and I think I wanted it to be about desire, for everything to have started there. Was I was being naive? Maybe she couldn't have a will or desires, because of her relationship to questions of sin, chastity and honour, or what, from an early age, she'd been told about men. François I's wife, Claude, had been seven years old when she was promised to him; his mother, Louise de Savoie, was eleven when she married; and by the time Marguerite de Navarre had turned seventeen she was forced to marry a duke in order to secure France's ownership of Armagnac.

The ties of royal women aren't necessarily representative of the norms of that time, because they were arrangements between states, in which their bodies were used as political currency, but they're the only ones we know anything about today, through history and their own voices, in the writings they left behind. I'd pored over pages about who had been married off to whom and who had taken which woman as a lover and which women excelled at scheming, as it were, and were, thanks to their sleeping with or being married to kings, involved in running their countries.

When Marguerite de Navarre was ten years old, her mother tried to broker a marriage between her and the

English prince Henry, who would become Henry VIII of the House of Tudor. While seeking out the facts, I stumbled upon a history blog dedicated to the TV series *The Tudors*, which said that Marguerite de Navarre featured in one of the episodes in the first season of the series: a fictional supporting character who bore her name and, according to the post, was only in the loosest sense based on the real woman.

I didn't watch much TV and I liked it when I had reason to do so for work. I immediately sought out *The Tudors* on Netflix and curled up with it on the living-room sofa. A few minutes into the episode I noticed that the person being depicted was an entirely different Marguerite de Navarre to the one I'd come to know through her writing and my research. The only point of recognition was her renowned beauty. In one of the first scenes, a member of court describes meeting her: 'I found her a beautiful young woman with a very sweet and yielding disposition. She confessed a great admiration for Your Majesty.' And this is how she is portrayed when she turns up as a guest at Henry VIII's court, with pillowy bosoms and glossy curls. The king's confidantes comment on her figure and he extends her an invitation, to which she responds with a bowed head and arch glances. In and of itself this wasn't particularly upsetting – there's nothing wrong with depicting a powerful or powerless young woman's desire to sleep with a king – but

to take an exceptionally powerful woman in history, perhaps the world's most powerful woman, and turn her into
one *maîtresse* among others? It was as though the series'
writers wanted to put Marguerite de Navarre in her place.
Not to mention the fact that the episode took place during or shortly after 24 February 1525, when François I was
imprisoned by Holy Roman Emperor Charles V in Pavia, to
where Navarre travelled in order to free him. The choice of
representation was confounding. How were women ever
supposed to feel equal to men if their histories were constantly being distorted?

When I read about Pavia and how Marguerite de Navarre had rescued her brother there, my interest in Emperor
Charles V or, rather, my interest in his mother, Joanna the
Mad, was also piqued, and I found myself searching for
books about her. So it often went. One name, one image,
one sentence and I'd stray from my subject. One thing led to
the next and it was difficult to keep everything in its bounds.

What also struck me about Marguerite de Navarre's depiction as merely a possible bedfellow for the Tudor king was
the irony of it, considering the influence she would exert
over the birth of Protestantism in England, which was one
of the key plot lines in the series, through her books and the
women in the Tudor dynasty who read them: Anne Boleyn,
Catherine Parr, Jane Seymour and Elizabeth I, among others.
I had recently discovered Elizabeth I's interpretation of

Navarre's poetry book *The Mirror of the Sinful Soul* (1531), a prose translation done by Elizabeth when she was only eleven years old, and which she had herself bound by hand. The photographed handwritten pages were so worn and aged that they were no longer legible in many places – the text large and neat, the letters on thin guide lines.

The 1,400-line poem was a sort of mystical monologue in which Marguerite de Navarre's literary 'I' investigates all the ways in which she has failed at living. I often pulled it up to read on my phone. It felt freeing and yet was a bit dispiriting because of how relevant this poem still felt, 500 years later; how all the as-yet unresolved questions made it resonate with some deep imperative. Perhaps it was the alienation of the female writer that enabled her appeal to reach freely through time and space. Like so many other works I'd read, *The Mirror of the Sinful Soul* seemed to have reached me on a sort of dark, subterranean journey through history. It had felt like no one but I could have caught sight of these works and I remembered thinking it was just as well, that perhaps bringing them to light would serve no purpose.

The Mirror of the Sinful Soul was Marguerite de Navarre's most controversial book and her Achilles heel. The Catholic Church deemed it blasphemous because in it she asserted that the only way to establish contact with God was to acknowledge your sins with full honesty. The concept spoke to me.

In one of the lines, she had written her first name, *Marguerite*, but Princess Elizabeth translated it as 'me', as though the poem were about her, which apparently she also thought it was. I was fascinated by how Elizabeth, at the age of eleven, had been drawn to poetry written by an adult woman; a queen and author speaking to a higher power about her sins and shortcomings. I couldn't help but wonder about the reasons why.

I now know they share common ground with the story I was working on, with punishment and quarantine, and with my own motives. But this is one path I won't follow.

Now when I look at the drawing and see all it contains, at least I think I can see it all; it's so clearly there, but in the beginning not much of it was visible. I spent a long time with the image, waiting for the scene to appear, piece by piece. The island and its inhabitants. The many lines and all the black marks and blotches bleeding into each other confused me. I kept losing myself in them. The etching became like an optical illusion slowly being solved.

What I first discerned was the island's notably square shape and the meandering coastline, the sea beyond, the waves and ships. Then I saw the leafy trees on the northern side and the wild caribou drawn on the far side of the stream that runs there. But everything revealed itself slowly, as if it were on a time delay.

My attention was drawn to the palm tree after I'd realised that, oddly enough, yes, it *was* a palm tree; to the dark fields in the background; and to what lay at its base – the sword, which I now know is the man's sword – and the flower-shaped object above it.

One afternoon, as I sat in bed with the image open on the computer, her figure suddenly appeared in its entirety and I saw her plain and clear in the middle of the drawing's lower half. It was a breakthrough, but also a disappointment. She looked so civilised, which wasn't at all how I'd pictured her. Her face wasn't rugged or animal-like in the least, but rather slim and elegant, with an introspective look to the eyes. Heavy eyelids. Her profile and guise recalled a Greek goddess: the posture, the broad shoulders, the unmarred fabric pleated around her legs. She was wearing her high-necked, long-sleeved dress and looked powerful and brave. In her arms was a long rifle aimed at a bear charging right towards her, while on the ground at her feet lay another bear.

I wondered what else I wasn't seeing in the picture and if it would be easier to make out the details if I could see it in person. I used a magnifying glass, but it didn't help. There was supposed to be a physical copy of *La Cosmographie Universelle* in the collections of the Kelly Library at the University of Toronto, and I assumed that's where Elizabeth Boyer had gone to view it, but Toronto wasn't exactly close to me. I had to content myself with the 1,046 pages of uploaded microfilm.

I thought if I printed it out, I might be able to make it clearer by using an image-editing program, but when scrolling through to the end of Thevet's book to quickly check how much I could zoom in and to see how the quality differed from the printout I had, which was out of focus and muddled, I couldn't find the right chapter. I saw a number of other etchings, all with the same dense lines and darkness, and several other islands, but I couldn't find the right one. The pages I was looking for were missing.

My first thought was that there had to be someone else who'd developed the same relationship to her as I had and who also didn't want to share her with others. I started fantasising about this person, how he or she was a sort of emotional copy of myself in another part of the world, in another profession, of another sex. Maybe a young man studying history with a focus on marine biology or navigation. I pictured his glasses and the way he looked, him speaking enthusiastically about the project, how his supervisor at some university in the north-eastern United States encouraged him over shared lunches. He also had a very supportive girlfriend . . . I could picture them all clearly.

When I came to my senses and started researching the issue, it turned out that Thevet's book, like Belleforest's, was much longer than I'd thought. *La Cosmographie Universelle* wasn't one book, but two. A work comprising over 4,000 pages. I soon found the second volume on a different website and quickly located the spread where the drawing was printed in the middle of a page, in the midst of the text and with a brief caption in the left-hand margin describing the picture. The caption made it sound as if what's happening to her is nothing out of the ordinary, just one normal occurrence among many.

Like the oil paintings I studied in the beginning, the etching was technically adept, but what struck me when I began to see the scene as a whole and understand it better was its relative simplicity, how the warped perspective made it seem more familiar and authentic than a naturalist portrait. That someone had drawn the island and her figure from her testimony – or as André Thevet recounted it, or if she had been the one to do so, suggested that it was a personal interpretation. Chief importance had not been placed on creating a faithful interpretation of reality, but rather the picture showed the maker's own assumptions or assertions – such as the presence of palm trees in North America. Or was the palm tree a recognised symbol for all strange continents yet to be discovered and conquered?

The drawing made me think that she must have liked being on the island, which would turn out to be true, but not in quite the way I was thinking and as the picture seemed to suggest. Perhaps the drawing is animated by the exploratory ideals of its era, but it could also be one of those visions of a 'strong woman' that had become popular in my lifetime and which was also probably part of the reason I was sitting there holding an A4 printout in my hands.

As I write this, I see that she likely would have wanted to project this image of herself. Because why would she have wanted to show herself to the world as she was, or as I was seeing her?

Shortly after she appeared to me in the lower part of the etching, I encountered another hurdle: a section of *A Colony of One* that made me feel even weaker than the idea that Marguerite de Navarre hadn't written Tale LXVII.

It was exactly the kind of information that often made me avoid researching my subjects too thoroughly. Presumably it can be summarised by the old maxim about never fact-checking a good story, but not only that. It also related to pure exhaustion: each complication I encountered in the documents I was writing and reading wore me out.

I'd brushed up against this fact myself, but I hadn't had the energy to take it on board because it overwhelmed me. Now it could no longer be avoided. There it was in black and white in the large book in front of me.

It was impossible to know who she was.

Not to say she hadn't existed, but exactly who she had been, exactly who she was, couldn't be determined. Her identity could not be proven because there were so many women with the same name back then: Marguerite was one of the most common first names, and 'de la Rocque', as she may have been called, with or without the *c* before the *q* or even with *ch*, was a very common surname. And because an apparent pact of silence between all interested parties had swept away every trace of her existence. She had been erased from history, except for a narrow space in the period between 1536 and 1544. And, as I read Boyer's books, this space narrowed even more.

There is a line between pointing out how a woman in history has been rendered invisible and contributing to her invisibility yourself, but where this line is drawn is not always clear. This often came to mind as I tried to find out more about her. Seeking out neglected female stories and trying to revive them has become quite a popular endeavour, and I have read many accounts by feminist writers on the women believed to have been left out of the historical record. But it seemed to me that the main reason for such accounts was that said feminists had not yet read or engaged with these women's work or what had already been written about them. A woman isn't necessarily forgotten just because she isn't mentioned in everyday debate or in the articles currently being shared on Facebook.

Marguerite de la Rocque (or however her name may have been spelled) didn't exist before Jean-François de la Rocque de Roberval tried to kill her. And after that, her identity was concealed in order to protect him and the other men involved, allowing them to walk free, and so it remained hidden throughout the centuries, making it no longer possible to tell which among the women of her time she had been.

Elizabeth Boyer presented three candidates in *A Colony of One*. One of them was the woman who was sworn in as a *seigneureuse* in Amboise and who today seems to be considered the right person. But Boyer wrote her off because she, in contrast to how I'd imagined it, was too old to have been a minor in the early 1540s when Roberval is said to have become her guardian. This woman's assets also lay too far from Nontron, where Thevet was thought to have met her and therefore assumed to be the place from where she hailed. Moreover, a woman with such large land holdings would hardly have had reason to embark on a perilous journey across the Atlantic. A woman with that sort of life would never have weathered what she had, so Boyer posits.

In this way, perhaps Boyer's view was more realistic than mine. She was imagining someone who from the start was cut from the right cloth, but clearly I preferred the idea of transformation: at first she didn't have it in her, but it had come to her, a previously unimaginable strength. Was this my immersion in modern, commercial film – the idea that the main character must change? They rarely changed in my books. Or at least that's what people usually said, and I found no reason to contradict them.

Elizabeth Boyer's final argument was that there was nothing to suggest that this Marguerite was related to Jean-François de la Rocque de Roberval. But according to Wikipedia, which I'd started consulting more often, she was in possession of yet another region, Pontpoint, which she owned together with him. This would speak to them being related after all, and also to him having a clear motive for his actions: if she disappeared, her holdings would pass to him, as long as she didn't die by his hand.

Pontpoint was mentioned once in *A Colony of One*, but it said nothing about Jean-François de la Rocque de Roberval and Marguerite de la Rocque owning it together. Had later researchers discovered something Boyer missed, a connection that hadn't yet been clarified in the early 1980s when she was writing her book? For me, it was yet another supervening difficulty. I no longer had the energy to consider what this would mean for me; I felt tired just thinking about having to delve into the historical research that might be available now, and relay Boyer's puzzle accordingly. It seemed strenuous, but it wasn't only that. I was still having such difficulty concentrating, and the worst part was that it wasn't exclusive to writing or reading about this topic. It applied to everything: novels, poetry collections, even news articles. I always read a number of books simultaneously, and when I found one I liked a lot, I got so attached to it I had a hard time finishing it. I had taken to leaving the last ten or twenty pages unread.

Besides which, there didn't seem to be anything new to discover. Or perhaps I'd decided that was so, to let myself off more easily. I wrote a few emails to people who seemed to be authorities in the field, soliciting help. Meanwhile, I saw the advantage in not being able to point to a person in history and identify her. For example, it could only be a good thing if she didn't have any relatives who might put forward an opinion about how she was being represented or that she was being written about at all in the first place. Yet I felt that I had been robbed of something, as though the object of a desire I sensed but couldn't understand had been snatched away from me right as I was catching sight of it. Why was her identity so important; why did it have so much meaning? It's not like I could pick up the phone and call her, if only I knew who she was – or that I'd even have wanted to, had it been an option.

I'd written to the editors of the Canadian history site I was using as a reference to ask for an explanation of their reasoning and for the source that establishes her identity. Perhaps a new state of affairs had indeed been brought to light since Boyer wrote her book, even if I hadn't seen anything that suggested there was ongoing research into the subject. There was a contact form on the page and there I posed my question. I was in New York at the time, to participate in a literary festival. Even though I had a full schedule, I kept devoting my time to her instead.

Later that night I went out with my American publisher. Everywhere was crowded, especially the Soho restaurant she'd picked for us, which was decorated like a classic French brasserie and, as always, was full. It was after my last appearance at the festival: I'd done a reading in a sandwich shop in lower Manhattan and had read a short piece that made up the final part of a story that four authors from four different parts of the world had written together. Each one had received the first sentence to jump off from, which had also been the last sentence in the previous piece, written by someone else. I had come to understand that authors did this kind of thing all the time, just as they participated in events with others, taught students or held workshops. For me, all of this was alien and taxing, and it was a relief when it was over.

A table opened up as soon as we arrived. We ordered and talked about everything that had happened since we'd last seen each other, and when my editor asked how the novel was going, the one with the tree, I explained that I'd had to put it aside; since I started working on this project, I couldn't get back into it.

I talked about my research into Marguerite and the script that I'd now agreed to develop into a television series instead, because people had started watching more TV than films. People were watching more TV series than news as well, devoting greater time to this than to anything else, and with a laugh the editor reminded me that TV series were the new novel. Even so, she added, this didn't mean that the novel as a form couldn't also be 'the new novel'.

'Everything takes its course,' she said. 'What you're saying sounds completely reasonable. And you know that the book you started will still be there once you've gotten this out of you. Then you can do whatever you want with it.'

She leaned forwards and asked if this wasn't going to be a book as well and I told it like it was. At first I had felt so liberated to, for once, be working on something I didn't also want to turn into a book, but now it seemed inevitable. It could no longer be helped. What I'd been so invested in when we'd last met seemed empty and meaningless now that I knew I would soon be able to return to Marguerite, and I couldn't start anything new, anything other than this.

The editor listened and nodded slowly. She was always so understanding and, like several of my other editors, she made me feel that my actions were normal, that what I was busying myself with was, well, *reasonable*, as she said, which gifted me a sense of calm. It removed some of the guilt, relieved it a bit at least. For a moment I felt like a person with a normal job, a normal life.

While I was talking about what I was up to, it had hit me that the feeling I'd had at the start perhaps hadn't been liberation at all, but rather a sign of its opposite: something I was comforting myself with in order to be able to endure not writing what I wanted to write. If I had shared these thoughts, she'd probably have been able to help me put it all in perspective, but I didn't say anything. Instead I took out my phone and pulled up the picture of the island and another spread from *La Cosmographie Universelle* that I'd also saved.

She looked at them for a long time, and when she reached over the small tray of oysters between us to hand me back my phone, she said there was one thing I should do before my departure. 'Go to the library at Bryant Park,' she said. 'They have a significant collection of old maps from various regions. I'm almost convinced there'd be something for you there. If you have time.'

When we finished eating, she told me about projects she was working on. In my mind's eye, the authors she was talking about popped up like a slide show. Each was a wonder of discipline, focus and talent, reading and parsing big material quickly and with ease. Their books were important and they felt no remorse about the relationship of their writing to everything else in their lives.

I envied them.

We left the restaurant, walked a few blocks and parted at a corner by one of the avenues. She was heading uptown, and I walked on alone through southern Manhattan.

Compared to the north, the autumn in New York was something else. The air was mild and fragrant and the pavements were full of people on their way to bars and restaurants and karaoke booths. I'd hardly expected a reply from the editors of the Canadian history site, but by the time I'd opened my laptop at the desk in my hotel room, an email had arrived.

The man writing informed me that he was out of the country at the moment, just like me then, and so couldn't say for sure, but he was almost certain the source was André Thevet. I'd expected as much. But Thevet didn't mention which regions were in Marguerite's possession, or what she was doing in 1536, in either of his books: *La Cosmographie Universelle* nor *Le Grand Insulaire*. In addition to her name, her first name, all he wrote in *La Cosmographie Universelle* was that she was a young noblewoman, a *demoiselle* (upon first reading the word I didn't know it was the origin of *mademoiselle*), and a 'very close relative' to Jean-François de la Rocque de Roberval, and that she was someone whom Roberval 'greatly respected and to whom he confided all his affairs, because she was of his blood'.

I started drafting a response. I made an effort to gather and formulate my most important lines of questioning: how did they know that the Marguerite de la Rocque who had sworn the oath in Amboise was in fact the woman in question? There were so many women with that name living at that time in those places, after all. And who was their source regarding her kinship with Roberval, or them co-owning Pontpoint? I also explained why I wanted to know.

When I was done, I reread the email and had second thoughts. I deleted every word. I didn't dare send it.

THE NEXT DAY was my last in New York. I had breakfast at a Ukrainian diner in the East Village with a friend and her young daughter. We talked about what it was like living with a child in a studio on the top floor of a nineteenth-century building without an elevator in the middle of Manhattan – 'Let's just say I don't really need to go out for a run these days' – and then I walked some twenty blocks up Fifth Avenue to the New York Public Library, as my editor had instructed.

I went through the main entrance with its grand maxims about literature; mottos hewn in stone came across as so anachronistic that what they described seemed to take on a new guise, as though reading and language no longer related to the cognitive but had become mystical, as though using the library for research was on a par with visiting one of the many clairvoyants in the city, who enticed with offers of reading the future in your palm.

After lining up for the security guard and letting him peer into my bag, which contained nothing but a charger for my phone, the programme for the PEN America World Voices Festival and two different lipsticks, I found the map department behind a small café in the corner of the Fifth Avenue entrance hall.

Inside, it was quiet and almost empty: a couple of people were sunk into reading chairs over by the window and, behind the information desk on one of the short ends of the room, a librarian was flipping through a card index. I walked up to the desk and asked her if they had anything by André Thevet. She was my age or a bit older – I'd often found myself thinking that other people were older than I when they were the same age or younger – and with a certain languor she showed me to a corner of the room filled with shelves of giant blue plastic folders.

This was the catalogue.

I looked up Thevet and found a typewritten entry in one column: *Le Nouveau Monde Découvert et Illustre de Nostre Temps* – A. Thevet, 1575. Had this been part of *La Cosmographie Universelle*? The librarian said she could issue me with a library card and order the map from the stacks but it would take until the afternoon to retrieve it. She gave me a form and a pencil, and once I'd filled it out, I thanked her and left.

Outside it was hot and sunny. I walked a few blocks uptown to 48th Street where I knew breadfruit was sold from a cart outside the entrance of one of the commercial skyscrapers. It was the middle of the lunch rush. Two men were loading up styrofoam boxes with food, which they were handing out to the people lined up on the pavement: bankers and office workers. Most people were either talking on their phones or with each other, and a number of them were switching between standard English and a patois I couldn't understand. The women were wearing short skirts and high-heeled shoes and I wondered what it meant to them, being women with nice shoes and jobs in Manhattan. If they had longed for this, imagined it for themselves. After a while, my turn came; the fruit's charred skin was peeled off and its hot flesh was cut up in front of me. I was given my box and took it back to the park and sat down by one of the green garden tables in the shadow of the library.

The taste was exactly as I remembered it and, like on all the other occasions I'd eaten breadfruit, I thought of when I first saw the word, in Daniel Defoe's *Robinson Crusoe*, the first book we were asked to read in school. My copy was very old and worn, with small ink illustrations of Robinson and Friday and all their tasks on the desert island. I put down the plastic fork and knife to take a picture of the food in the styrofoam box, but the second I was hovering my phone over it, a man appeared beside me and snatched the box, cutlery and all, and ran off through the park. I turned to watch him, got up and saw him slow down at the crossing and continue at a slower pace along Fifth Avenue, a slice of breadfruit in one hand.

I just stood there. No one around me had noticed what had happened. I picked up the napkin left behind on the empty table and crumpled it up. It would be a while yet before I could see the map, but I started walking towards the stone steps that led to the library doors. People had flocked to the wide stairs and were climbing them with something like reverence. Some were carrying computer bags and books and looked like they were about to sit down to work in the large reading room on the top floor, while others might have just been going to peer into the famous room with its long rows of desks and reading lamps. The reading room was split in two: in one part tourists were welcome to drink in the atmosphere and view the interior; in the other you could sit in peace without risk of interruption or being captured in a photo and posted online.

The Map Division on the first floor wasn't beautiful in the same way, but photography was restricted there too, and it was silent and calm inside, even though it had filled up with people. The only sound was of clacking keys, pages turning, the scratch of pen on paper. There was an air of deep concentration. I went to the desk and the librarian handed me a pair of thin, white cotton gloves, which I immediately slipped on. She showed me to a spot by the long reading table that was positioned so she would have a full view of what was going on from there. When I sat down, she went over to one of the book carts next to her desk and picked up a large portfolio, which I assumed contained the map. Slowly and with a hint of solemnity, she carried it through the room, and when she reached me, placed it gently before me on the table. The scent of dust and old paper wafted up at me. I drew a deep breath and sneezed. The smell took me by surprise. The librarian didn't flinch. She just leaned closer, unknotted the fabric strap holding the portfolio together and with a sweeping gesture opened it, exposing its contents.

Le Nouveau Monde Découvert et Illustre de Nostre Temps was over half a metre wide and almost as tall, with brown woodcut on linen. I wondered if there was a chance that André Thevet himself had held this copy in his hands and I wondered how he'd felt in the years he'd occupied himself with drawing the world's every corner, what he thought about his work and himself.

He had divided the New World into territories respective to colonial powers: *lieues Italiques, lieues Francoyza, lieues Marinza* – Italy, France, Spain. Upon closer inspection of the map, I noticed that his idea of the American continents resembled my own. The most notable difference was that Argentina's southernmost tip wasn't particularly pointed, but round, like a large peninsula, and to its left was a glimpse of New Guinea that, for some reason, he'd rendered giant.

As far back as I can remember, I'd wondered how the first cartographers worked. How could they create such clear pictures of the earth? Even today it was hard to understand how everything fitted together, the countries and the oceans and islands and mountains, and for those of us who still had freedom of movement, our ability to cross the globe with such speed was breathtaking. But if our maps now were as similar to maps then, as they seemed, perhaps ours weren't particularly accurate either, but rather a product of estimation and guesswork. I suppose that's what science is, developing theories and believing in them until disproven.

The island is on the northern part of the Gulf of Saint Lawrence, an estuary between Newfoundland and Labrador, and Québec, that is as large as an ocean and constitutes the outlet from the Great Lakes and the river that bears the name of the gulf. Jacques Cartier had passed it on his first exploratory voyage. He spied the island on Saint Martha's Day, 29 July 1534, and because he followed the General Roman Calendar in his naming of what he saw in the new land, he christened it, along with the surrounding islands and islets, 'Martha'– Lazarus's sister, who in the New Testament hears Jesus say that he is the Resurrection and the Life after Lazarus dies and is raised from the dead. (As a child I remember thinking the stories about resurrection were terrible, the obvious lie of them: the only truth they contained was that of an objection to the irreversible.)

To the west, the estuary meets the river beyond the strait named after Jacques Cartier. I wondered if Jean-François de la Rocque de Roberval might have wished that this narrow passage bore his name instead. He was the one who gave the island the name it most commonly

had in the records: Île des Démons. He encouraged Jean
Alfonse de Saintonge and André Thevet and all other navigators and cartographers to rename it thus in order to
warn approaching mariners of the evil spirits and demons
that inhabited it. French fishing boats had trawled for
cod around there since the 1400s and perhaps the island
already had this reputation – or perhaps he was the one
who had imparted it then, so no one would go ashore and
discover what he'd left behind.

I have yet to find a map where the island is called
Île Sainte Marthe. On *Le Nouveau Monde Découvert et Illustre de Nostre Temps,* which lay before me, there was no
island by this name, nor was there an Île des Démons or
Île de Roberval, as Thevet would later call it. Of course
this made sense: why would this tiny island appear on
Thevet's map of the entire new world? But this didn't
occur to me as I sat in the library, bewitched by being
able to hold this map.

Once my eyes had adjusted to the way the names were
written in that faded, scrolling style, my gaze fell on one Île
des Diables, just south of Greenland. Now, I can clearly see
that this island lies too far north-east and isn't even inside
the estuary, but I couldn't before. I'd confused it with Île
des Démons, thinking this was its name because it's what I
wanted to see, because it was all about this island for me, as
though it was the centre of everything.

On the plane home and for several days after I'd returned from New York I read about the Île des Diables in Google Books and in other text archives until, one overcast morning, I was sitting around at home, flipping aimlessly through the notes in *A Colony of One*, and caught sight of Elizabeth Boyer's copy of *Le Routier de Jean Alphonse, de Xantoigne*, which showed the course he had set to get to the island when sailing up through the Gulf of Saint Lawrence. For some reason this is what allowed me to discover my mistake – and that I was far from alone in making it: several other researchers and authors had written about the island in question as Île des Diables instead of Île des Démons.

To be honest, this pleased me. I thought it would lead everyone else who might be looking for her astray. Earlier, I had found an unsigned map dated 1556, on which the name Île des Démons is clearly printed and illustrated with devils and angels and naked people seeking shelter in simple huts. The land south of the island is labelled Terra Nova, the land on the other side as Terra de Labrador, and in the water on the east side a 'Levante' ocean current is marked out by a large sea creature.

The island would be given other names, of which one was crucial to the development of her story. At least that's what I believe. Nowadays it has been given yet another; again it has been named after a European nobleman, an English count and military officer whose connection to it is tenuous. After Jean-François de la Rocque de Roberval's death, Thevet chose to mark it as Île de Roberval on his maps. In his writings, the reason he gives is his deep bond of friendship with Roberval and because he, Roberval, was the one to first set foot on the island. And yes, this may have been the case. Maybe Roberval really did approach it in the little boat, wade towards the beach with the crew and the women, only to then overtake them so he would be first, climbing ashore and planting the French flag in some crevice.

But this isn't how I imagine it.

I think of my version of this event, the one so real to me it hardly could have transpired any other way, and then I think of what Cartier wrote in a letter home during his first voyage, wondering if 'the New World' wasn't the wrong moniker, that it should have instead been called a land of 'stone and fearsome cliffs' (and I wonder also what it was like for those who had to carry letters like these home, those who had to turn right back around as soon as they had finally arrived).

In his writings, André Thevet states again and again that he's straying from his subject, and I drew so much satisfaction from reading this. In the collection of documents titled *Le Grande Insulaire*, which can be found at the Bibliothèque National de France in Paris, he devotes many paragraphs to the evil spirits on the island: how they took on the form of wild animals or manifested as horrifying visions that tormented her. I wonder if he dwelled on this to demonstrate the hell she was subjected to, or to support Roberval's statement and maintain the rumour that the island was haunted. Science was just beginning to win ground from religious belief and magical thinking, and it was common to see scientific research devoted to supernatural matters. Thevet wrote that he didn't question that souls could return and reveal themselves to the living, but he wanted to leave this matter to theologists and other experts in the field:

> Better that I should deal with other matters, also very difficult, as it is my pleasure to discover points to the readers which will rejoice and interest them but I stray too far from my subject.

I could picture it: his pen, *quill*, his thoughts that in the midst of reports and calculations flowed like sheets of rain down a mountain face. I imagined the writing room where he sat, the pressure of the tip on the page, the forward-slanted script I recognise from all of the manuscripts, the lilting, swirling 'S' that has since vanished from written language.

But his subject was the uncharted continent, not she who managed to survive there. His subject was the island. He wrote that it was beautiful and as cold as an island could be, populated only by demons and wild beasts. Even though he too had never been there, images of it recur throughout his writing, as they did for me. He dreamed himself away to that place in the same way I did, if for other reasons.

AT FIRST THE frequency with which Thevet referred to Jean-François de la Rocque de Roberval as his close friend seemed odd. His apparent reverence provoked me. He would interject a comment on what a good man Roberval was in the middle of a sentence about his cruel treatment of her, or others. For example: on a single day in the colony in New France, which he had christened Francy-Roy in honour of his friend François I, he hanged six people and put a gang in leg irons and flogged them until the blood flowed, even though they were his 'favourites'.

I imagined that Thevet had the captain's back and of course this upset me: not only because it was an image of the patriarchy but also because, through my reading, I had my own relationship with Thevet. I didn't want to accept that his loyalty to Roberval was greater than his compassion for her, in spite of everything he knew, everything she told him during their meeting in Nontron. Not that it surprised me; on the contrary, it was the most natural assumption for me to make. But once I'd read him and read a great deal about him, I didn't want to see it that way. His lengthy descriptions of landmasses and oceans, everything on this planet, had made me want to trust him. His writing had made me want to think well of him.

This was how a narrative voice worked for me, in spite of all I had learned about unreliable narrators. I liked reading what he wrote about the island and so I wanted him to condemn Roberval. Meanwhile, I'd started wondering why it was so important to me, and if he had in fact supported his friend's actions. Wasn't there a chance that Thevet could be Roberval's friend and still think that what he was doing was wrong?

I found André Thevet's map online, and also a dark etching depicting him, which I printed out and put up on the wall alongside my other pictures. He was bearded and dressed in some sort of draped garment. In front of him was a globe on a pedestal, one of his hands was open, as though he were carefully underscoring what he'd just said, and his other hand was holding what looked like pliers, but which I assumed was a navigational instrument, and was resting on the globe. He seemed to be lecturing and looked earnest, as though he was troubled by the subject.

Because of my difficulties concentrating, I struggled to engage with the literature I needed to read about the French Renaissance and Age of Exploration, but I noticed that the more I did and the more I familiarised myself with that period in general, the more realistic and useful my interpretations of what was written about her became. I realised just how limited my view of Thevet's chapter in *La Cosmographie Universelle* had been. The two other sources were short stories based on real events, and I read them as fiction, with all this implied, but when it came to André Thevet it was as though I had forgotten how every text is shaped by its context and must be read with that in mind. It was as though I had lost my sensitivity and suddenly had the same need for things to be over-explained that irked me so in others. I had mixed up truth and authenticity, as though the fact that the source texts were historical relics had led me to read them literally.

Just because it was on the page in black and white didn't mean it was true. That André Thevet took every opportunity to honour Jean-François de la Rocque de Roberval didn't mean that was really what he wanted to do. He may well have felt forced to, in order to get away with writing what he did – all that his manuscript also conveyed.

Looking at the portrait of Thevet again, something so obvious occurred to me: whereas today it would be considered unthinkable, there must have been much greater sympathy for what Roberval was doing back then. After all the time I'd spent on this project, it was remarkable how much I hadn't considered. *La Cosmographie Universelle* wasn't printed until after Roberval's death, but while André Thevet was writing the book, he could very well have been afraid of being punished for it, by Roberval himself or by one of the institutions protecting him. Thevet could also have feared that what he disclosed about his meeting with her and what she told him would be used to punish her. The aim of his assurances of friendship and loyalty may have been to protect her. Roberval's exemption from criticism was probably reasonable, because the man acted entirely upon his own authority. She would never be given redress for what he had done to her – her very survival was against all odds: it was a fact that upset all physical laws and for him to be aware of this could further endanger her life.

For me, André Thevet's article with its many detailed descriptions of things that might seem irrelevant – the evil spirits, for instance – was imbued with value, no matter his reason for writing it. I knew I'd never come close to knowing his motivations and it wasn't a given that I would have been able to understand them even if I had been alive back when his books were published and had read them. That is, *if* I'd been able to read, as a woman in those times.

In the same paragraph that Thevet wrote about his honourable friend, he first mentions her, saying that among those who travelled across the ocean with the captain was a noblewoman. Did she know he'd done that? Had she read the book, read about herself and seen her portrait in it? Perhaps redress for her was meaningless to him in his writing; perhaps she really was just one witness among others on whom he relied when it came to the New World, because he himself had not been there. Was her experience merely a digression that nevertheless needed to be thoroughly investigated for what it might have revealed about the conditions there?

But his text is a kind of reparation for her, intentional or not: the invocation of the island and of her physical presence on it, her name and her title; the descriptions of animals and nature, of demons; the naming of things she surrounded herself with, the other people, the timeline of key events, however crudely or briefly they were described; the rendering of her words, prayers and dreams. He is the only one who wrote her name.

Still my gaze is drawn to the same part of the black etching. To the point right in front of the little log cabin, which she'd told Thevet they had built together, where a small oval shape has been drawn on the ground. What's lying there is swaddled, caterpillar-shaped and appears to be unmoving.

I write that it begins with death. It's death that takes her father and death that drives the conviction to take over the world and tame its wildness. It's 15 January 1541 when Jean-François de la Rocque de Roberval is appointed chief in command of the latest expedition to New France and viceroy, the highest authority in the whole of the new territory. The document outlining his commission is more than twice as long as the one Jacques Cartier received a few years prior. It expresses King François I's wish to become acquainted with the uninhabited and empty foreign lands that lie across the water, and also the great confidence he has in Roberval who, though entirely lacking in formal qualifications, is described as the only person for the job. The document praises his ambition, his faithful service to Church and Crown, his sound judgement, loyalty and many other commendable deeds.

Roberval is to take over from Jacques Cartier on his third voyage. He is to travel beyond Newfoundland, to what is called Candia or Canada, to found a colony that the king hopes will bring in substantial earnings as well as eternal glory and honour for the Divine. The Crown's emissaries are to rescue the savages from the barbarism, irrationality and ignorance in which they are mired, save them and bestow upon them French Christian sons. Jean-François de la Rocque de Roberval is to bring a considerable entourage and shall have unchecked power in the colony, on land and at sea, and over every Frenchman who sets foot there. He shall build castles and churches and spread the holy Catholic faith.

I write that this final point is a small price to pay. My assumption was that he wouldn't have a problem setting aside his own religious convictions for a mission such as this one, but then I saw that André Thevet ascribed Roberval's toughness as a commander to Reformism, to him being a Calvinist. I wondered if this should be read as a general description of a brutal and power-hungry character or if Jean-François de la Rocque de Roberval, despite the religious conflicts, might have taken the opportunity to spread his own faith, and got the colonists to avow themselves to it.

His fleet consisted of three newly built ships: *La Vallentyne*, *Sainte-Anne* and *Marye*. The names of some of the noblemen who chose to follow him to sea are also on record. According to one preserved list they were called Guinecourt, Sainterre, L'Espiney, Noir Fontaine, Dieu Lamont, De La Brosse, Frete, Francis de Mire, La Salle and Royeze.

On the same night that I started reading about the ship and encountered the names, I went to a dinner party at the home of some friends I hadn't seen in a while. I didn't visit people much anymore because it was hard to get away and I didn't like having anything scheduled beyond my work and my daily tasks. Still, I would occasionally decide to socialise. On this evening, I'd left the children at home, but when I arrived I saw that all the other guests had brought their children along. They were lying under the table and playing while their parents drank wine and talked about their jobs. A man sitting on a kitchen chair with a two-year-old in his lap asked me what I was writing, if I'd be coming out with anything new soon. I tried to get out of answering the question. If the others responded enthusiastically, I knew it would make me feel insufficient because I imagined that I could only disappoint them, but there was also the risk that they'd start talking about what they'd be writing if they were authors, or about how wonderful it must be to be one – 'Imagine being able to sit around all day plumbing your own depths,' as a woman had once put it to me, smiling as though it were the best thing imaginable.

Neither did I want to be reminded of what a fantastic story this was, because it would only make me think about how I was ruining it. I was self-absorbed in the way that fear-driven people become, but I hadn't considered the fact that all authors are self-absorbed because our inner lives come to dominate and because we are working only with ourselves. There was always a chance that I'd have a meaningful experience if I shared my endeavour with others. It had happened before.

So, I explained, in brief. The man thought it strange that the French were so obsessed with the New World: what were they going to do with Canada when they already had France? *Kanata.* I didn't understand what he meant, but didn't have a chance to ask a follow-up question; he'd already started talking about a trip he had taken to a nudist camp in Carcassonne and I thought about a conflict that had long interested me, the one between naturists who believe their way of life to be superior and those who want to be naked because it turns them on.

'Carcassonne, you said?' I asked, just to be sure.

'Yes,' he said.

How strange that he would mention this particular city. It was Roberval's birthplace. Was this yet another sign? (Was I a fool searching for signs and thinking I was

seeing them everywhere?) The conversation around the
dinner table moved on, to French colonialism in Africa
and South East Asia, and no one seemed especially keen
to hear more about her. This probably had more to do
with my storytelling than anything else. I couldn't even
recount a tale as fantastic as this one in an engaging way,
and I tried not to think about what this suggested regarding my ability to write it.

After dinner I had to hurry home. I had felt hot inside the
apartment with all the people and the cooking, but outside
an icy rain was falling. It was raw and pitch-black, even
though it wasn't late. If I hurried I might make it home
in time to read to the children before they fell asleep. I
wrapped my scarf around my head and jogged home, eyes
on the pavement, watching out for slippery patches of
half-rotten leaves.

Inside the apartment it was almost as dark as it was outside. The rain pounded against the window panes and a cold
draught blew through the windows and across the floors.
The children were already asleep in their beds. My husband
was also asleep, on the sofa, his reading glasses in one hand
and the Kafka biography he was reading open on his chest.
I took my iPad from the coffee table and lay down next to
him, pulled a throw over me and nuzzled in close to soak
up the heat from his large body. He didn't notice me as he
was in a deep sleep. I continued reading about how work

was conducted on a ship such as *La Vallentyne*, what they ate, how they slept and such. I thought about the conditions on those ships. I wondered how small her berth was, how they all fitted and how the others had managed, the ones who didn't even have berths but had to sleep in shifts on bunks. I read that during the crossing Roberval had stored the drinking water in such a way that it soon spoiled, and when the water supply had to be poured out, there was only cider left to drink. How vile it must have been on those ships when all on board, people and animals alike, were drunk.

I considered that the man I'd met at the dinner must have meant that France was so wonderful that the idea of wanting to leave it seemed strange. But in the early 1540s the country was sunk in misery; large parts of it were lawless, riven by religious strife. There was no order, no safety and no sense that any of it would improve.

No one but the king and his inner circle could have enjoyed living there, but setting out to sea was by no means a desirable alternative. It's likely that the noblemen who followed Roberval across the Atlantic did so because they were forced to, either because he had some sort of hold on them or because François I, in his bid to modernise the country, had confiscated their land so they felt forced to acquire more in order to reinstate their families' status.

But what about her? I'd given so much thought to why she went along and what it said about who she was. It had

almost become the most central point for me. I wondered if
her life before the crossing had been so full of hardship that
it made travelling across a furious sea for two months in the
company of hundreds of strange men seem appealing, or if
she too had been forced to go, by Roberval or by a dearth of
other options, or if the nameless man had swayed her.

But the bigger question for me was if something inside
her may have awakened. It's what I had pictured most often
at the beginning: some shapeless imperative that tugged at
her, an inescapable force that drove her towards a renowned
darkness, a focal point of sorts that she wanted to see with
her own eyes. I had often lamented the question that is forever being asked about women, about the women in my
books and about women in general when they strike out on
their own: *is she a victim or is she a strong woman?* But what I
noticed when I started on this was that I seemed to be suffering from the same impulse to denounce and differentiate.
Inside the question of her desire lay a key to how she would
be constructed, who she was and who we the viewer wanted
her to be, and what this would say about us.

As long as I had been reading books, my view of women
had hindered my reading, and as long as I had been writing,
I'd tried to tackle this: my idea that women were better than
men, my wish for this to be true even when it clearly wasn't.
I write 'my' but it was a general idea, recurring everywhere,
serving as a contrast to, but also a confirmation of, gender

inequality. When I became an author myself, I saw how this view contaminated my writing, making it untrue and not based on experience, but in spite of this I couldn't make a clean break. Reconciling this within myself wasn't enough because it was a general tendency, a broad recurring gesture in society.

For so long I'd wanted to see her in a certain light and had hoped that what there was to discover about her would support my idea of who she was, would show that she was who I wanted her to be. This didn't only apply to her, of course, but the young woman as a character. I could never fully grasp if it was just me, not that I was alone in my thinking, but that these thoughts, the system in which they operated, seemed more dominant from my perspective because of my work and the questions and discussions they usually gave rise to, or if a young woman's inner life – her subject, her will and motives – really was seen, by society or in our collective unconscious, as inherently exotic?

There was a tension in the space between the lingering clichés about women and lived experience – it was tantalising and unwieldy. Even for me, even though I'd engaged with this topic for so long, I was as susceptible as anyone else to notions about women as good, unwitting victims in a man's world; weak, selfless, in need of saving, and I was just as susceptible to the dictate to behave in a certain way (and in this book, *to depict women in a certain way*) that perpetuates such notions.

My thoughts were also charged by the idea that she may well have wanted to go to the New World for the same reasons as Jean-François de la Rocque de Roberval. She wouldn't have needed to hide the fact that she could read or write from him, but she'd hidden it from others, and if Roberval shared François I's passion for literature, culture and modernity, perhaps he also embraced the nascent humanist ideals that the Renaissance had sown about education for women – a tiny minority of women, but women nonetheless. Perhaps it's as Thevet suggests: he respected her. (It had been a long time since I heard any man say he 'respected' a woman, but I recalled how embarrassing it sounded to me, as though he didn't actually respect women but could imagine making an exception.) And if this was the case, he may well have allowed her to partake in his preparations for the trip, all the plans and calculations and meetings with people who wanted to go along or who were to be convinced to do so. Perhaps she had long been interested in her guardian's project, an innocent who entered his life and was animated by his great dream – the dream I now considered to be evil. She saw the items in his room, held them in her hands and listened to his stories and plans, read his reports, studied his nautical charts and maps, perhaps followed him to Amboise to meet the Iroquois king, Donnacona, who Jacques Cartier had taken there. I imagined an empty vessel of a young woman, allowing herself to be filled with his ideas, letting them take root in her.

After receiving his commission, Roberval had devoted his time to persuading the right people to join him on this journey: skilled tradesmen, experienced sailors, famous men such as Jean Alfonse. It's possible that she shared in this work, listening at the door to his study or even being invited to sit in on their meetings. It's possible that she wanted to travel with him across the ocean in spite of the danger and it's possible that the trip had the same meaning for the both of them, that the evil of exploration and violence belonged to her as well. Long had this bothered me, but after my visit to Roberval, I cared less. I wasn't frightened off by the thought of her perhaps wanting to claim the New World as much and as brutally as the men involved. I no longer required her to be better than them. I'm not even sure I hoped she would be, not once.

Of all those who would be persuaded to take part in the voyage, Jean Alfonse de Saintonge was the most important. That he joined them was crucial. He had sailed along the American coast towards Mexico and was the period's great authority on navigation and sailmaking. In contrast to Jacques Cartier and André Thevet, Alfonse was better known during his lifetime than after, and it seemed typical that he wasn't rewarded in the same way as they were. Maybe I've taken it a bit for granted that the role he played in this drama was the one I'd assumed he had played.

In Paris I had thought of him every day, on our way back to the hotel and passing by the little Rue de Saintonge, right behind the Comme des Garçons shop, and I had wondered if it had been named after him and what sort of power was ensuring that I was forever moving inside an echo of this story. Only on the last night did it strike me that the street, like Rue de Bretagne right next to it, where the bistro we went to was, had been named after a region, and Jean Alfonse wasn't two first names but a first and last name and de Saintonge was a demonym that had been added on. It was so obvious, really.

Alfonse was supposed to guide the three ships, using Cartier's nautical charts, to the fortress in St John's, which was on the same latitude as La Rochelle and the reason for it being called New France. After that, they'd sail north to the place where they intended to build the colony.

I'd tried to find images of ships from this period so that I could see what they looked like, but there were none, which was an absence also addressed by Elizabeth Boyer in her book. Here in Stockholm, I wondered if I should visit the Wasa Museum across town and have a look at the seventeenth-century warship housed there, but if I did I should take the children with me, mixing business with pleasure, so to speak – even if it was unclear which was which.

Almost every time I tried to find out facts about Roberval's fleet, I'd end up plotting our trip. I visited the museum's homepage and checked the opening hours, calculated when we'd have to leave school in order to make it in time and perused the range of guided tours.

Now, as I was lying next to my sleeping husband, I had the urge to do so again, but then an article caught my eye, on how shipbuilding had changed during the second half of the 1500s. As the rain hammered down ever harder on the windows, I read on, and after a couple of paragraphs it was clear the changes had been so comprehensive that there would be no point in looking at a ship one hundred years younger than the one in which she'd travelled.

I've probably never been as troubled as I was that autumn, by thoughts and impulses, by the memories rising up inside me and revealing themselves. With each minute my brain seemed to be trying to get me to shift focus to something that would be easier and more agreeable than what I was in the middle of doing.

I had constant thoughts of the summer and those hot, beautiful days in Paris. I pictured my daughter sitting on the ground and sunning herself against the wall next to the tower in Roberval and I remembered slowing down for a second to look at her face, the freckles that had emerged over the weekend, how beautiful they were and how quickly they darkened, multiplied and spread.

When she felt me looking at her, she'd opened her eyes and taken out one of her white earbuds as if to ask me what I wanted. I shook my head but kept looking at her. She turned her face back to the sun and shut her eyes. Except for the dull hum from the road, all was silent. It was late in the afternoon, but still hot. Aymen had taken off his jacket and unbuttoned the collar of his white shirt and was leaning on the car under the chestnut tree. I walked up to the tower and squinted at the sculpture atop the black roof – the faces, their expressions, looking out over all four points of the compass.

My daughter got up and walked along the footpath towards the parking area. I stayed where I was and turned back to the tower. Out of the corner of my eye I saw her dancing on the grass, her phone in her hand, doing choreography from a music video. The sun shone on the rocks, glittering with minerals yet matted by dust from the road and the ground and the mortar; my shadow fell across them like a dark streak and I think that's when I remembered. It must have been how the sunshine was grazing the pale stones in the wall. The wall and the tower and being so close to them. I felt like an idiot when I realised it. I hadn't been in Paris the summer I was the same age as my daughter was now, but in La Rochelle. How could I have forgotten? How was it possible for me to have read and written the city's name so often over the course of this project and not have remembered it properly?

My mother had been of the opinion that children shouldn't be taken on holidays because they wouldn't remember them later in life anyway, and now I concede that she was right, at least in part. But that year she must have thought I was old enough. It was a road trip: we had driven along the coast through Normandy and Brittany and on to the Poitou-Charentes region. In the mornings we stopped and bought coffee and those greasy pain au raisin that flaked as you ate them and used to only be available in France. I'd been allowed to keep the change each time I ran in to do the shopping in the bakeries along the way, and when we reached La Rochelle, I had enough money to buy matches and a packet of cigarettes. To avoid detection, I'd gone down to the harbour. It was crowded around the medieval citadel by the inlet, but at the edge of the fortress behind one of its two towers was a ledge with a bench facing the water, which was exactly where Roberval's fleet had been anchored in anticipation of departure, but I didn't know that then.

Out there on the narrow ledge, no one could see me and all I could see was the ocean, the old fortress rising from the glittering blue water and the Atlantic horizon beyond it. The wind was blowing head on, but somehow I managed to strike a match and light one of the cigarettes. A strong but unspeakable desire rose inside me. I remember thinking that I would never forget this moment and I haven't. I had preserved the memory, but it was so deeply fixed in me and my own narrative that I hadn't come to think of it in this context.

I leaned against the tower and brought my face to it, feeling the stone against my hair. I thought about her and him and longed to be perfused with them as I stood there, but what came instead was a sudden homesickness, the anticipation of tomorrow when I'd be sitting at my computer and writing about them, reconstructing their movements at this place, but also my own at this moment. Only then would this become real to me.

THERE IS NOTHING that confirms her existence before the day Jean-François de la Rocque de Roberval's fleet sets off from the harbour in La Rochelle. It is 16 April 1542. I like this date. That it is written down. It's something I can hold onto, it's the lone anchor for the days and years that lead up to today, to me.

Not even then is her name to be found, but I know she's there.

I write that she is standing next to Roberval at the top of the fortress and looking out over the harbour and the ocean and down at the work going on around three docked ships. The quayside below is swarming. He points things out and explains. Agricultural machines, tools and provisions are being carried aboard. There are sailors, ploughmen, millers, carpenters and smiths; many of them have been in La Rochelle for days, weeks, waiting.

Like Jacques Cartier before him, Roberval had been allowed to take with him prison inmates; it was the only way to get enough people on the expedition. It had surprised me that he, who is described as a total pedant with regard to his project, seemed to have such a liberal view of breeding. I presumed that his faith was what had made him willing to populate his country with criminals, his assumption being that people could be saved and shaped. But then I read an article about the convict travellers of the colonial era, in which was described the 'auditions' Roberval organised in the years before the expedition. Forty or so people had been employed to travel around and select the right sort of prisoner; preferably noblemen who had happened to have been sentenced for some sort of war crime, manslaughter or illegal duel – and he had personally visited institutions near Paris and the town of Roberval, to prevent them from offloading their worst prisoners – cannibals and serial killers – on him.

The chosen convicts had travelled in chains by foot, from villages and cities far from the coast, and were held in detention centres near the harbour. They would be shipped alongside the animals on the ships: ten pigs, twenty horses and twenty cows, four bulls, one hundred sheep and one hundred goats.

I wondered if he felt like Noah with his ark as he stood there with her by his side, watching everything. Or if she'd said as much to him, to his delight. Yes, that's how it was.

I HAD A counter that showed how many days, hours, minutes and seconds had passed since that day. Whenever I had to

enter the date I was forced to look it up in one of my books,
because I hadn't noted it down properly. Why was this always
the case? Because I was avoiding anything that underscored
the research element of this project, I resisted collecting and
organising the essential data. Time after time I filled books
with notes and Post-its only to tear them out and toss them
away, even though I knew I'd have to mark those places with
new notes.

I never really wanted to commit my research to paper.
Instead I imagined immersing myself in the material, becoming one with the facts, then all I'd have to do was write. I
wanted her to arise in me. I had no desire to see that we were
two separate people, and her continued subjugation was the
link that spanned the time between us; here I was, a person
in a position to exert power over her. Yet another one.

But this method was also a way to avoid making decisions,
thinking I'd keep it all in my head and remember it, and that
what I didn't remember wasn't worth putting in.

HER MENSTRUATION WAS a practical detail on which I dwelled.
I had read how a poultice of dried toad could ease menstrual
cramps and how cramps were ideally to be endured because
they, like woman's labour pains, were God's punishment for
the sin and lechery she bore inside her. Predictably there was
a passage about the Tudor dynasty – everything to do with

the 1500s seemed to be about the Tudors today – regarding an order of a certain type of Dutch cotton for Elizabeth I's household linens, and in one coeval translation of the Bible there is mention of cloth rags being used as pads.

It must have been awful, but menstruation is still an issue in the world today – wherever access to feminine hygiene products is lacking, for various reasons. I watched a short television documentary on it and read about a researcher who had mapped where women couldn't work or even leave their homes because of the shame of walking around with a bloody rag between their legs. However, in the historical archives, I found nothing more on the subject, which galled me until I concluded that it didn't matter. I didn't need to know more about it because she wouldn't even have been menstruating. At most her period would have come twice on the boat, but once is more likely because menstrual cycles were longer and less regular back then, as so many suffered from malnutrition and exhaustion. Where had I read that? Probably some blog I'd come across while looking for ways to improve my own health, raise my energy levels. Later, she wouldn't have had her period at all. So, there was one circumstance that might have played into her hands, I thought.

Even if it was theoretically possible for the bleeding to have resumed, considering the course of events it's highly unlikely it did. Really, this wasn't significant – it wasn't like she wouldn't have known other pains or have felt physically

unwell otherwise, but I was fixated on her menstruation.
Now, I see that the reason for this must have been because
my own periods had stopped.

I can see why, too, the reasons for that. It frightens me
as much now, but not like it did when I thought I was suffering from some obscure women's illness or was entering
menopause. Brushing my teeth in the evenings, I looked at
my reflection in the mirror: the sun-bleached parts of my
hair seemed ashen and my face tinged with grey. It was
leaner now and the skin seemed to sag from my cheekbones
and under my eyes. My hands appeared to be the hands of
an old woman; the skin was loose over the knuckles and
deep wrinkles ran in parallel lines between them, like the
bark between the branches of a tree. I'd always thought
I'd enjoy ageing, the transformation into something other
than what I had once been, but now that it was happening,
I could only take it as an expression of something dreadful.

I took it to be yet another omen, that it was in this very spot, in this harbour, in this city. I had thought it a remarkable coincidence, but as I'm writing these words, I know it isn't remarkable, it's logical. I had visited this place before, as had many others; the tourist buses in the harbour car park; the tour guides cutting a path, their folded umbrellas raised overhead so they could be followed. It is logical to have been in these places and to later return, that it is towards them that we direct our attention.

I write that she follows Jean-François de la Rocque de Roberval across the gangplank and on board *La Vallentyne*. In some places it says that 800 men went aboard on this day in April, in others 200 men. She is the only woman. (Well, Damienne is by her side, but she doesn't count.) Standing on the flagship's deck, he is the first person she sees. I write that his name is X, because he doesn't have a name and I couldn't pick one for him; whatever I chose seemed to be charged with my own thoughts of who he should be. I write that he is taller than the other men and that she sees him in their midst before he lays eyes on her, and when he takes her hand he is holding the cithern in the other, his fingers closed around the instrument's slender neck.

The rest I don't know.

But afterward, when the ship sets out from the harbour and she is alone in her berth, she takes the book out of her hair and lies with it in her hands. She flips through it, fingers damp with sweat, and reads the words on the thin pages and then presses the tiny book to her, to her chest, as though she could suppress and still what had been unleashed in her. She hears the activity on deck, her guardian's commands – and then another voice that might belong to him, the man without a name.

She may have seen him on several previous occasions but this is the first time the sight of him unleashes something that renders volatile what was once fixed – she no longer knows anything about God or herself or her beliefs.

In the beginning I thought of it as hypocrisy and a double standard but I think this is to underestimate her and to underestimate every dimension of hypocrisy and double standards in a human mind. She need not have been the least bit insecure. It's fully possible for her to have loved God and still know all about the sensations washing over her after the encounter with him, and after their every subsequent encounter.

My publisher had put me in touch with a professor of French at Stockholm University who was able to help me interpret

sections of François de Belleforest's novella. After email-
ing him my initial questions, he'd written back to confirm
that François de Belleforest, too, had not named the man
anywhere in the over-forty-page-long story. Instead he
describes him as an aristocrat and a troubadour who sang
and played songs of love and death on his lute (I thought
it was a cithern – according to Thevet, it's a cithern), and
compares him to the mythological knight Tristan. In his
email, the professor explained that the narrative voice
claims at first not to know the man's name, but by the end
of the story changes his mind about who the story is about:
'Regrettably, he knows their names.'

So Belleforest knew. I'd gotten it into my head that Marguerite de Navarre did as well. Had she been acquainted
with the man and his family and wanted to protect them,
as she seems to have wanted to protect her? Was Belleforest
acquainted with him too, perhaps from his time at the court
in Pau, and was of the same mind, and if so had also met her?
Did they all know each other?

All the other names are mentioned at some point in at least
one of the other sources, but when it comes to him, it's as if
they'd agreed to stay silent. Maybe his name is among those
on the list of Roberval's companions, maybe it's on another.
François de Belleforest refers to him as the 'aristocrat' or 'the
French nobleman'; Marguerite de Navarre refers to him as
'the lover', 'the husband', or a craftsman. At the start of the

entry in *La Cosmographie Universelle*, André Thevet presents him as 'a sturdy fellow' and then calls him 'the gentleman', 'this gentleman', and 'the said young man'. I think his repetition underscores the deliberate preservation of anonymity. It is almost as though he wishes to call attention to it, or even protest against it. But why would he want to?

I'll just call him 'the man' now, or the man without a name. I wonder about him and think of the word *man*, of how under certain circumstances it still embarrasses me, but also that he, to her, isn't really a man in the first instance, but rather someone who reminds her of herself and who she recognises on sight, the moment before the crew parts before her, the captain and Damienne. Before he turns around to look at her.

I write that it happens on the ship. It's probably a sort of nod to the mood, the first storm, the great vessel careening and lurching over a seemingly endless, threatening sea. But it could just as well be seen as a nod to the perspective that has led to us not knowing anything about her today, that she only begins to exist on the day Jean-François de la Rocque de Roberval sets sail with her.

Not even I allow her to exist prior to this.

I write that it is their first cithern lesson. They sit on deck and around them work continues as usual, but they're unfazed by it. First he sings the song for her and then he shows her how it's done, how to hold the instrument in her hands. She is embarrassed, but he approaches his task with the utmost seriousness. Entertaining and educating the viceroy's ward is important, but so is bringing music to the New World. Her fingers must land in the right place: he takes them between his and moves them on the strings, positioning her fingertips one by one. Damienne looks between them and the sea. At that moment, the storm is no more than a shadow in the distant sky, just above the waterline. There's a shift in the air, first a cooling of daylight, then the heavy gloom of clouds covering sun. After that, darkness, the wind and whip of rain. It happens so fast. The man without a name takes hold of her with one hand and Damienne with the other – she's still clutching the instrument. They hurl themselves into her cabin and crowd inside, playing on as the storm ravages the deck and the men outside, forcing them to their knees; Jean-François de la Rocque de Roberval stands at the helm shouting his orders.

I imagine that he's also shouting to God. That he considers a storm to be a reasonable test and a form of dialogue between the two of them. I can picture his stance, his grip on the helm, his face tilted to the sky, and when the ship shakes it looks as though it's his doing, as though he were rattling it with all his might.

This is when Damienne runs from the cabin, hand over her mouth, and this is when it happens, the second they find themselves alone. She grabs hold of him, his upper arm, his shoulder, the crook of his elbow. At first all he does is hold her as the ship careens and flies across the waves. The boat's movements and their movements, it's as if the storm were driving them, making her grab at him, pulling him towards her. The rumbling storm drowns out their noise and the eclipse conceals their bodies in the cabin. The cithern is on the floor.

Damienne stands outside, clutching a manrope, doubled over; vomit spills from her mouth and is blown back onto her, clinging like a spider web to her kirtle, the deck and her feet already wet with the driving rain, and the ocean's mighty waves crashing over the railing. She stands there, gripping a stay, her thin body bent and heaving with sea-sickness. She is trying to collect herself so she can go back inside, but by the time she does, it's too late. The damage has already been done.

Their ill-fated union – I think this is how André Thevet describes it – was like a catastrophe she wanted to yield to. I romanticised it as much as anyone else who'd written about it in the intervening centuries. I imagine her experiencing atonement as the catastrophe pulls her along. A force that takes hold of her and sweeps her away, into the wide blue yonder, helpless, and because she is helpless, because there is nothing with which to resist, a sort of relief arises. It lies in the physical sensation itself, in the movement, as something larger that embraces her as it embraces him, from a different direction.

I hadn't read the New Testament, but I knew it said that flesh leads to fornication, impurity, misery, and those who yield to it will not inherit the kingdom of God. God aside, it was hard for me to comprehend how she dared. The idea of the erotic as a complication and threat with the potential to nullify all else wasn't as vivid to me right then as it had been during my first introduction to her. Increasingly I couldn't really relate to the idea of an urge that arises, perhaps as an innocent longing, and then turns against her and takes her in its grip. I could feel the feeling but I couldn't as easily imagine the ease with which everything of importance could be risked for it alone.

It made me think that the loyalty between her and Jean-François de la Rocque de Roberval was perhaps not mutual, that perhaps she didn't return the intimacy he'd claimed there was between them, or that André Thevet's assertion of it was groundless. It could have also been that she didn't have the same faith in the colonial project, she didn't think she had much to lose, and she loved the man without a name in such a way that justified anything they did together – at least up until the point he was no longer there, when he was nowhere to be found.

They could have first met that day in La Rochelle, but they might also have met during one of the royal hunts at Château de Roberval or even earlier, in southern France, perhaps when they were children, had their families known each other. Perhaps their love, like her, had existed long before. For a while I tried to convince myself that this was of no importance, and on one level it wasn't, but at the same time the question of their relationship is crucial to how we view her. I wanted to know where they first slept together because I wanted to picture it, but also because I thought the answer to my questions might lie in knowing.

Thevet wrote that the man without a name had come along on the journey 'more for love of the aforesaid noblewoman than for service to the king or respect for the captain, which was made most apparent later on'. Could it be that he hadn't actually needed to go with them, but only did because of her? Or did she go for his sake, because he had convinced her to or because she wanted to? This was less believable. According to Thevet, the man was the driving force:

> While at sea, this gentleman did not fail to approach the aforesaid noblewoman so privately that in spite of the perils and dangers which are offered to those who travel at the mercy of the winds, they played their game together so well that they went beyond promises or mere words.

It could have been something she said during her interview with Thevet because she wished it had been so – because she felt ashamed of herself or because it was how it had to be. Maybe they hadn't even spoken about it, but rather it was an assumption as natural as any other. And what did the word 'love' even mean in André Thevet's book? Had this sturdy, nameless nobleman seen her at a distance in one of the castles, considered her as a possible object of courtship – or had they met, seen each other, touched each other?

I write that she grows accustomed to the sea. The bodies of water ebbing and flowing. Their might as they raise the boat, sending her upwards, forwards and releasing, sometimes making her catch air and drop back down. The line between the ocean and sky is present whichever way she looks; there is disorientation when it's no longer there, when all around her are the dark walls of a storm or the milky misting fog.

On one side of my notebook it says: *Does she get used to the men, too?* I was thinking about all of the men on board, but him as well. At first it might have frightened her to be with all of those men. Does this mean I'm turning her into an innocent little girl, or is it a function of remembering what it was like to be so possessed for the first time?

I remember one of my first editors, the comments he pencilled into the margins of a printout of the first chapter of the first draft of one of my earlier novels: *Rephrase questions as statements. Avoid asking too many questions.*

According to Jean Alfonse's calculations, the journey across the ocean would take sixty days. She keeps out of the way at first; sitting in the pilothouse as he and Roberval set their course and predict the weather and wind and how to change course if necessary, their options for escape if they end up in a storm the ships can't handle. Roberval walks in and out of the cabin. He takes in the crew and the ocean. When all is calm, he searches for signs of change; the weather is unpredictable but so are the men. Everything he does on board, every movement, is a display of mastery over them, but he can do nothing about the sea. It simply *is*, impossible to tame. In contrast to what he and Jean Alfonse seem to believe when their instruments and navigational charts are between them, it can't be controlled. It is unamenable to reason, but they seem to believe that God will protect them.

For a long time I took this to be the reason – Roberval having to placate God since she had awakened his rage – but that was probably naive of me. A well-meaning, atheistic interpretation. Now I'm more inclined to think it was as my friend had once suggested: he'd already made his plans for her, and bringing her along on this journey was a sort of ulti-mate solution to all of his problems. Her crime presented him with an opportunity to do as he pleased with her. Did he think the Divine had unexpectedly come to his aid, or was this the motive for him wanting the man without a name to teach her the cithern, because he had sensed that something might happen between them that would give him reason to jettison her from the expedition?

I didn't want to believe it at first. Perhaps I didn't want to believe he could be so calculating and cruel, but more so because, in this case, she wouldn't be alone in driving this story: it would become unromantic, or somewhere along the way I'd presupposed that Roberval wouldn't willingly cede her to another man.

I so very much wanted to know who was driving the events forwards and couldn't shake the idea that identifying the person whose thoughts and actions were behind them was possible. But there was also the matter of me wanting to try and understand what her relationship to sex and love was and what she knew about them, whether or not she had been a virgin and what concepts such as 'virgin' and 'chastity' meant to her. I, too, was mired in the question of whether to see her as a subject or object, as if she could only be one or the other, or one at a time.

Her constant presence must have made Roberval a bit uncomfortable. Jean Alfonse shows her his navigational

instruments and allows her to examine them: quadrants
and tables, astrolabes and alidades, of which he has written
in *L'Hydrographie d'un Découvreur du Canada et les Pilotes de
Pantagruel*, the book in which he also notes that navigators
at this time don't exactly keep their eyes on the stars and if
one of them did, then it would be unintentional. He tells her
about Homer and Oceanus and the compass-like object that
Leif Erikson and the Vikings had called a *solskuggafjol*, about
how to calculate azimuths and about the very first maps – not
maps of the land and sea, but of the starry night sky. It must
have roused feelings of guilt and ambivalence towards her –
even he must have been capable of such emotions – and this
created yet another possibility; this was why, to get her out
of his sight and avoid his emotions, he had asked the man
without a name to show her his instrument and to teach her
how to play it.

I don't actually remember if I'd read that he asked him to or
if I made it up. From quite early on it was like this: I wasn't sure
what I'd taken from my sources, or from elsewhere, and what
was from my own imagination. I tended to see Jean Alfonse de
Saintonge as Jean-François de la Rocque de Roberval's antith-
esis. Was it because I needed there to be one? As though, deep
down, I was hoping someone would be a bit nice to her. I hadn't
thought it would be like this from the start, but the deeper I got
into the story, the more often I was filled with a yearning for
balance, a wish for someone in this tale to be good.

I still think that Jean Alfonse must have had a hand in how things panned out. That *Le Routier de Jean Alfonse*, the navigational document he was working on throughout the voyage and which he published shortly after his return to Paris, was proof of his loyalty to her. It was there in black and white. I was more sure of Jean Alfonse than the man without a name. When it came to *him*, I was enchanted by love at first, but increasingly I only felt sure of my uncertainty.

It is said that the strongest emotions are and have always been universal, but how can one be sure? I wondered which thoughts and dreams were available to her, and if the thoughts and dreams came from the deep unknown that resides in each of us or from the wide expanse of what we all share, what is steered by everything that has been and all that we've invented – if the two things are even different, or if it's possible to speak of them separately.

I didn't know if attraction felt the same for her as it had for me at her age, but I could imagine the triumph of the erotic along with the couple becoming incautious because of the conviction that 'if it feels right, it's right'. Or couldn't they keep quiet about it? I read women's love poems from the Middle Ages and the Renaissance – Marie de France, Christine de Pizan, Marguerite de Navarre, Louise Labé

and a few others – and was taken by a sentence in Labé's
Débat de Folie et d'Amour from 1555:

> *Brief: La plus grand plaisir qui soit l'amour est d'en parler.*
> Second best to love is talking about it.

It would have been no surprise if one of them had discussed
it with someone else during those eight weeks at sea. That
is, someone other than Damienne. Or if Damienne had. But
that would probably have been for other reasons, such as
her feeling like the situation had slipped out of her hands
and she needed help, which would have been completely
understandable. She had one job as a chaperone, and she had
failed. And so the rumour spread through the ship.

Perhaps they were discovered early on, perhaps when
they docked for the first time. In *Histoires Tragiques* François
de Belleforest also avoids naming Jean-François de la Rocque
de Roberval – 'out of respect'. In the story, it doesn't take
long for the captain to find out that she – introduced there as
his sister – has given herself to one of the noblemen aboard
the ship. André Thevet also wrote that Roberval had been
informed about his ward's scandalous affair early in the voyage, but he'd 'discreetly and wisely' bided his time and kept
his rage contained.

Even if he had designs on betraying her in a worse way
than she had betrayed him, he was furious with her. She'd

been ignorant of his plans, she couldn't have known that he had anything but good intentions for her and she did put trust in the fact that he was her guardian, and yet she had risked everything by dishonouring and bringing shame upon him and his fleet – on all of France, really – the Church and the colonial project. It was as though she had dragged the entire blessed earth through the mud with her sins, as though she feared no god.

The biggest tree in front of Roberval's castle was larger than the chestnut and taller than the tower. I'd read that he had built his tower to free up capital ahead of the trip, but he'd clearly also done this to secure his own greatness for posterity, so the world would know of and remember him – and as such my presence there meant I was falling in line with his wishes.

Above my head the crown of the tree extended like a roof. I couldn't see the sky through the dense foliage. The sun's rays couldn't cut through the canopy, but they illuminated it with an even shine that meant I was looking up into a blazing bright green – I was trying to figure out how to describe it – a green so alive and yet so unnatural.

I wouldn't be able to find the words.

I came closer to the wall, ran my hand along it and followed it to the curve of the tower wall. I felt the pale stones. The mortar between them crumbled under my touch. I was so close, but it didn't feel like I was, as though there were an almost visible distance between my faculties of comprehension and the tower and the wall beside me. I backed up,

paced the lawn and photographed the tower and the walls
from various angles. By doing this, I thought I was co-opting
these relics, but the camera was a boundary I was erecting
between myself and them. I knew I wouldn't be able to experience them fully until I was back home, writing about them
and, in this way, reaching my consciousness towards them
anew. But then I wouldn't want to look at the pictures. I'd
just want to write, I thought, and would shy away from the
idea of getting the photos up and seeing what they showed
me, thus risking that they'd force me to describe this all in a
different way.

My daughter was walking around in the distance with
her white earbuds in her ears and her phone held out in
front of her. She was staring right into the screen and I wondered what she really thought about the thing we were
doing right now. The thing that I was doing that she'd been
invited to join. (Join in on.) If she even cared, she probably
had other ideas about what we were doing: *hopefully* she did.
Her childhood was so unlike mine. It calmed me to think
that she wouldn't need to endure growing up in the same
way I thought I'd had to – but I wondered if thoughts like
this diminished her. Weren't such assurances exactly what
divorced people from reality and made us repeat our parents' mistakes, because we couldn't see ourselves through
our children's eyes, see how their upbringings were entirely
their own and not correctives for the ones we had?

Aymen waited for us, for me, leaning against his car, legs wide with one foot in front of the other. He was smoking and talking on the phone in Arabic with the same giddy smile he'd been wearing throughout the drive. His tone was expectant and he kept bursting into laughter. I wondered what was delighting him so.

I wanted more pictures of the tower and took my phone out again. It was cracked along the top of the screen. I'd dropped it on the street a few days earlier outside the pawn shop, waiting to be let in so that I could sell some broken jewellery I didn't wear anymore and, I found out, would have cost more to repair than what I could get for it. Now the phone was in a case that I kept having to adjust because it obstructed the camera lens, but I felt unexpectedly pleased whenever I saw the crack, pleased with my decision not to repair it.

I'd started thinking about money more often. Since 'author' had become a sort of job for me, an occupation I devoted all my working hours to, I'd been fixated on economics. I couldn't let go of the idea that every krona deposited in my bank account was an opportunity to keep writing, while every krona withdrawn, by the same logic, would make it harder. With each passing month I became less willing to spend my money because I never knew if or when I'd make more. I tried to keep one eye on my expenditures and sometimes thought that if I'd never started buying expensive smartphones that needed constant repair or replacement, my personal finances would have been in better shape. But, above all, it was about my ability to concentrate. I convinced myself that my focus would have been less splintered now. I'd have been able to read more, write better, work longer hours and be more satisfied with what I was achieving. I'd have found out more about the French Renaissance and the Reformation, more about her, more about what I was doing.

I often hear people complaining about how hard it is to sustain the level of concentration needed to read and write and blaming it on their phones, and for this reason I'd once bought a flip phone and put away my iPhone, but the result was a series of misunderstandings that were only cleared up once I turned my smartphone back on and saw all the messages that hadn't reached me: rescheduled meetings, door codes I'd waited in vain for from parents of my children's friends, reminders about homework and field trips.

I'd long been of the opinion that the telephone had an essential function. It brought me to a kind of midpoint that I needed to be near because it was necessary for a writer, a person working so privately and living so alone, to try and be present in her time, conceptually at least, but it had become clearer that I couldn't really look at it this way. Technology took me to a midpoint, but the more it evolved, the clearer it became that this point was but one among billions of midpoints on earth, a point inside each and every one. It had nothing to do with a centre as I imagined it.

Then I noticed the shape of the leaves. Only then, in that moment.

How had I failed to see this earlier? It was a maple. I didn't know anything about trees and didn't know the life span of a maple, how quickly they grew, if it was feasible that this one had stood here then, and neither did I know about its origin. Had Roberval brought the maple to Canada or had he brought them over here from there?

From one second to the next, the rush I felt at the sight of the green leaves' edges was replaced with a fatigue in the face of everything I wanted to know. The details. All these seemingly never-ending details that kept revealing themselves to me and which all seemed so full of meaning. It was almost overpowering.

She wasn't really the only woman on the boat. Just because it's what writers have written doesn't mean it's true; it just means she was the only woman who counted. After the first storm, she roams the ship, to occupy herself and to try to evade her wicked thoughts and the sin nestling inside her. The exhausted men sit at their posts. It is silent, and the grey water is so still that she wants to reach for it, as though it could be touched.

She descends further and further, and as she approaches one of the cargo holds below deck, she hears an animal sound, but at closer range she hears that it's women's voices whispering and moaning. She stands still and listens and hears single words and hissing and iron against wet wood as they move around the cell. I found an article citing a letter from Jean-François de la Rocque de Roberval to one of the institutions, which included a list of eighteen convicts whose release he wished to request so he could take them on this trip. Of them four were women. I read their names, their ages and the crimes for which they were serving their sentences:

Mariette de la Tappye, 40, convicted of murdering her son-in-law. Cassette Chapu, 40, convicted of abuse and fornication. Antoinette de Paradis, 25, convicted of theft. Jehanne de la Veerye, 30, convicted of having sold her daughter.

I write that discovering them in the hold brings her relief. They will be of service and not her – because I imagine that's what she'd been thinking. Their bodies and their reproductive organs. She was the only woman of noble birth, but this isn't to say she wasn't first and foremost seen as a brood sow. It only meant that more thorough arrangements about how she was to be handled, as such, would be required. It is said that on one of the other ships was another girl, an eighteen-year-old named Mondyne Boispie, who was accompanying a prisoner who had been promised freedom in the new land. But even having found out about Mondyne, she'd struggled to piece together how all the new country's French sons were to be born with a bunch of men and only two women. Was there any chance she didn't view this as a threat?

It would be interesting if the man without a name left a comfortable existence behind in order to be close to her – but this isn't essential to my idea of who he is. His intentions seem a bit less relevant simply because he is a man and so his sexuality is seen as a more integrated part of his personality, as well as of secondary importance: not decisive, but a natural urge like any other a man might have. He could be driven by lust but it wouldn't render him incapable of differentiating between lust and logic. Different rules apply to a woman.

Because these women's issues were a kind of constant companion, I didn't quite see that they weren't what the story was primarily about. They weren't why it was holding me in a vice-like grip, and with each passing day making me more frightened of what was to come.

My daughter had squatted down on the gravel near Aymen's parked car. She was holding her phone straight out in front of her, eyes fixed on the screen. Aymen was on the other side of the car now, smoking a fresh cigarette and seemed to be watching the road, where cars were passing by with increasing frequency. I wondered if we should go soon. I looked at the clock on my phone. There was time. I could take another wander along the castle wall. It was still drawing me in, enticing and challenging me. Aymen didn't seem to have anything against waiting around in the sun for a little longer. This made me happy. Had he complained or seemed the least bit bored or impatient I could have easily imagined breaking this off and leaving sooner for his sake, even though I didn't know him, and nor did I have any such obligations towards him, but because it had always distressed me to be the source of someone else's disapproval.

I lingered on the grass between the gravel pitch and the castle and then started slowly walking closer. I wanted to stretch the moment out but I also didn't want us to be in a rush for our flight later. I'd rather not travel at all; I'd rather not ever leave this place. As long as I was here I was an author doing something concrete that her work apparently demanded of her and a parent on an outing with one of her children, but once I returned home and got going with writing and the everyday life surrounding it, I'd be a person making countless mistakes, doubting herself and her every action and constantly trying to find a little extra time for this or that.

And that's how it was.

DURING THE SUBSEQUENT half year of winter, I feared the darkness more than I can remember having feared it before. It heaved its full weight on me, as though it wanted to stifle and end me once and for all. I've always thought there was an ongoing fight between light and dark inside me. Sometimes I thought the light had been in me from the start and the darkness was what had found its way in, sometimes vice versa, but the location of the power struggle shifted, so that the forces seemed mostly to lie outside me. I was just a vessel through which they moved.

I had several author appearances booked in various countries. Among other places I was going to California, *sunny California*, and I really wanted to believe what people in our part of the world say: it's possible to charge your body with sunlight, like charging a battery. I spent the plane journey writing. I'd had a few good writing days and I think perhaps the very knowledge that I would soon get to see that south-western American sunshine had made that happen: the sun that nourished oranges and avocados and lit up canyons and beaches, everything that all of us who've never been there have heard about. The very thought of the sun began to rouse me from my hibernation, as though its rays were already shining on me.

This must've been one of the reasons – for once being consumed with being able to write – that I hadn't prepared for the trip, or maybe it was because I usually over-planned and I'd started trying to take each day more as it came, as this seemed like the better approach. I don't know. Of course I'd looked through my itinerary and at Google Maps, where I'd picked out a few places I wanted to visit if I had the time, but I hadn't done much more and so I was unprepared for what awaited me in San Francisco.

Throughout the airport were TV screens showing news reports about the devastation and rescue work happening as a result of the fires that had been ravaging the vineyards in Napa Valley for days and had spread unchecked, devastating the land and annihilating the crops. People were evacuated, they'd lost everything they owned and a number had died. An older couple had refused to leave when the alarm sounded, and when the fire reached their house, they'd jumped into their pool where they had remained for hours. The news showed the footage they had filmed with their phones as they lay in the water – shaky pans of the house and garden, the fire a dark inferno overhead.

After I'd picked up my baggage and walked through the arrivals hall and, moments later, found myself in the backseat of the consul general's car driving into the city, I saw the sun. In the middle of that thick grey sky it sat, a faint glowing dot, a ruddy reflection of the fire. The smoke from the fires had settled like a lid over the day and a thick smog hung outside the car windows. The Golden Gate Bridge was barely visible as we drove past it and I felt ashamed for having yearned for the heat that had now turned against those who lived here.

I arrived at the hotel and installed myself in a room with a large bay window, the kind I'd seen in films and TV shows and so knew was as typical for San Francisco as the cable cars and the many steep hills. To keep awake and to adjust my rhythms to the time zone I visited the Uniqlo shop around the corner and bought new down jackets for the children and new, extra-warm long underwear for myself. When I got back to the room I had a sore throat. It made me nervous. I couldn't get sick and miss all of my engagements. I wrote an email asking to cancel the evening's activities, a dance performance and a dinner, in order to be well for the reading I was supposed to give the next day. I kept myself awake for a few hours by watching CNN and the debate about the term 'alternative facts' that had started circulating some six months earlier and which was still occupying the public; about fake news and the wall the new president had promised to build at the Mexican border in order to keep migrants out; and about what had actually led to a person like him being elected President of the United States.

I fell asleep with the baiting voices echoing in my head and the sense of failure that visited me whenever I felt unwell, because I had learned to demand that my body fall in line. However, when I woke up in the morning, my throat felt normal. I was so relieved that I practically bounded out of bed. I pulled on my gym shorts and sneakers, then rode the elevator down to the lobby, took a paper cup from a holder and filled it with coffee from the coffeemaker. I stepped onto the pavement. Looking down on the city, it was pitch black. I coughed. It was hot out but something was wrong; it was overcast again and the air burned and felt filthy somehow. It tore at my skin and chest. A fresh coughing fit overcame me. My throat was again raw and when I saw the large notice on the door to the hardware shop that was wall-to-wall with the hotel – WE'RE OUT OF MASKS – I realised I wasn't sick: the smoke from the fires outside the city was irritating my airways. I felt relieved but also worried.

I decided to go to City Lights bookshop, just to see it for myself, and to see if I could buy a breathing mask on the way. They couldn't be sold out everywhere.

Walking through a strange city in the morning was among the best things I knew, and I'd longed for the feeling it usually unleashed, but it didn't quite arrive this time. A faint smell hung in the air, like a mix of roasted chestnuts and burnt rubber, and at first there wasn't a person to be seen. The narrow streets and hills ahead were empty, and the only people I did see were the homeless sleeping against the building walls here and there, and tourists like me proceeding with caution. The sun was still the same feeble glowing red dot that had been in the sky upon arrival and the ghostly mood corresponded well with the overarching impression I had that something had gone wrong, that the world was being poisoned and everything was topsy-turvy.

I arrived at City Lights and spent a moment outside reading the signs in the window, which told the story of the bookshop's history and Lawrence Ferlinghetti and the Beat poets, and the shop as a symbol for 1960s counterculture. My interest in the Beats had largely been stoked by a short piece by Diane di Prima that I'd read in an anthology of female Beat poets. I had lent it to someone and never got it back, and if I were to find it now, her piece might not speak to me in the same way as it did then. On the contrary, it might make me think about myself, the much younger person I had been when I'd read it, and think less of her.

When I walked into the shop I went to the section dedicated to translated literature – presumably large for an

American bookshop and yet not really large at all – and I saw my novel on the shelves.

It was early in the day, but the shop was already full of people milling around the shelves, taking selfies, reading the small plaques about the shop's history that were nailed to the wall. Many people were taking books from the shelves, standing around and reading and flipping through them, but no one was at the cash register. I didn't see anyone buying books and didn't know if I was going to buy anything myself. I walked deeper into the shop and found myself in a back room where specialist books waiting to be marked down had been stacked in a corner. I sifted through one of the piles, imagining I might take pity on one of the books. The first one I saw was a dissertation on Allen Ginsberg's 'Howl' and next to it was a book about Hamsun, which I picked up, but put down the second I saw the words 'Rape and Writing' on the cover of a book sticking out near the bottom of the pile. It looked like my kind of thing.

I bent over and pulled out the book as carefully as I could. When I saw the full title, it startled me; the pile collapsed and books tumbled to the ground. *Rape and Writing in the* Heptaméron *of Marguerite de Navarre*. On the cover was the illustrated portrait of Marguerite de Navarre with her lapdog, but with the dog cropped out. The book was from 1991, by Patricia Francis Cholakian, an associate professor of French at Hamilton College in New York, and was described on the back cover as a literary analysis that by using psychoanalytic, semiotic and narratological perspectives was making new inroads into Marguerite de Navarre's short stories and how they could be understood relative to their time and to the frame story.

I sank down amidst the jumble of books on the floor, set the book in my lap, opened it and began to read.

Ever since I first heard about the island the thought of it has enticed me. An outcrop in the water far from where I was. The prevailing emptiness and the silence, sounds not directed at me and whose meaning I would never understand.

The solid landmasses surrounding the enormous gulf where the island lies had been named after what Jacques Cartier thought the 'savages' had called them. *Kanata*. In other words, she was by no means the only living person on the 'undiscovered' continent during those years: the Iroquois and the Inuit were also there; the island lay in the midst of their fairway, their nautical warpath. It was a matter of them not being viewed as human beings.

According to the documents that have been preserved, Roberval's fleet reaches St John's on 8 June 1542. When they sail into the estuary they encounter Cartier, who is on his way home after his third failed mission in North America. He had neither found the Northwest Passage nor the route to the mythical Saguénay, where blond, white warriors are said to have become rich from gold and furs many years before. The gems he had found had turned out to be worthless, and thirty or forty of his colonists had been killed by indigenous people. Roberval tried to get him to join them and continue the search for Saguénay, but Cartier sailed away under the cover of night, and the following day Roberval's fleet continued on towards the rivers and the land, heading for Cartier's abandoned fort at Royal-Charlesbourg, named after François I's son Charles, and what is today Cap-Rouge – a neighbourhood in Québec with red brick rental blocks and a shopping centre with a golf simulator.

It is hard to imagine a desert island. I populate it with my inner gaze. I write that, as they approach, it appears like a crushed mountain out in the grey water. It's summer, but summer near Newfoundland and Labrador, north of Nova Scotia. Jagged cliffs, some dense groves, a hollow as wide as a valley.

Roberval stands by the rudder with Jean Alfonse. She observes them at a slight distance from her spot on deck. Those two, who usually include her, haven't told her about this manoeuvre. Why are they steering into the archipelago when their course is set to continue west towards the river? From a distance she follows their movements. She watches Jean Alfonse point at skerries and islets and then to his chart, and Jean-François de la Rocque de Roberval shakes his head.

It is overcast and windy. The large ship has a good wind in its sails as it passes between the small islands scattered in the gulf. What happens next is that Roberval comes over to her. He moves through the crowd of men on the deck and hands her the little book. He must have dug it out from her things in the berth. She takes it and hides it in her dress. He disappears and his men approach her, they lift her up between them, several of them carry her away. She searches for the man without a name, but he is nowhere to be seen. The seamen carry her over the deck while the other men who have gathered look on in silence.

In the past weeks it is likely that she has become acquainted with several crew members and among them may have been some she'd come to view as friends, but it is unlikely that any of them would defend her. According to the 'Third Tale' in François de Belleforest's *Histoires Tragiques*, the crew is aware of the secret relationship and they don't like it. In the story the captain explains to his 'sister' that she is acting like a whore. And she protests: *No, I am not a streetwalker.* He says that he is in no way as cruel as she is ungrateful and this is why he's furnishing her with provisions and weapons and ammunition.

A skiff is slipped into the water, with rusks, arquebuses and gunpowder. I assume Jean-François de la Rocque de Roberval was careful to demonstrate that the purpose of this expulsion was to rebuke his ward, not to end her life, because if she were to die by his hand he wouldn't be able to inherit her assets. It was also an opportunity to make clear to the colonists who were to be under his rule that he would not hesitate to punish even the person closest to him.

During these trips I took that fall and winter, I realised that my increased access to light was more than an opportunity for me to write. The lessening of daylight in the southerly latitudes was an entirely different beast to the daily darkness in northerly ones, but still it implied confinement: the deep blue tones, their quick descent and the darkness that raised its walls and kept me from moving around freely in these new, strange places. I thought about all the times I had heard about the Nordic light, that cliché; how could I still not have seen that the north was a bright place – as well – what else was obvious about the world that I hadn't been able to take in? Which of nature's other powers was I unaware of?

From San Francisco I went on to Los Angeles. The fires had burned there too, in various places around the city, but they'd contained them more quickly, and when I stepped out of the arrivals hall, I could breathe normally. My lungs filled with the unfamiliar air: hot exhaust, cleaning products, cigarette smoke. I had a room in a vintage luxury hotel in Hollywood where I was meant to sit and write for a few days. The Chateau Marmont, referred to as The Chateau, was built like a medieval French castle, its towers and pinnacles sticking up behind the billboards on the boulevard.

When I arrived the receptionist told me that Marilyn Monroe had stayed in my room: she had lain in the bed I was to sleep in and in the petite powder pink bathtub in the bathroom. He told me about other stars who had stayed at the hotel and how certain guests made their bookings based on a room's particular history. As for me, I wasn't particularly drawn in by the movie-star glamour of which they made so much, but nonetheless the old building soon had a peculiar effect on me. Perhaps this came down to it being its own sort of bubble, where it was easy to imagine that all else had ceased to exist. The lobby was dusky no matter the hour and empty for the most part during the day; it had a stale smell and a floor that groaned when you crossed it. In the dark lobby bar was an old gramophone that always had a record on and doors that opened onto a paved inner courtyard, which reminded me of that book about Narnia I'd finally dug out and started reading to the kids. The courtyard resembled an old castle garden with its sculptures and deep stone benches, grapevines and ramblers, and had a dense lawn interlaid with thick flagstones, creating a chessboard pattern.

It was in the courtyard that the hotel's restaurant lay and at this time in the morning, when the air was heavy with the night's grey dew, I sat there writing. In the evenings my computer was set up on the desk in my room and I kept the tall windows open to the hum from below, and in the afternoons I read the Cholakian by the pool and was supplied with cigarettes by a man I recognised from a medical TV show that ran when I was a teenager and still living at home. I used to sit on the floor in front of the television set after school eating cornflakes while watching it. He looked exactly the same now – even though he was wearing a baseball cap and sunglasses, I'd recognised him at once.

There was a lot I wanted to see in LA. I took a few small outings to various places, but I spent most of my time at the hotel. There was something strange about it, but I couldn't put my finger on what.

On my last night, a journalist came to interview me about the novel. We met in the restaurant. She was wearing a red shift dress that was draped at the waist and her slender white arms and hands were tattooed with small black marks and symbols.

'I'm assuming you've noticed how all the women here are young,' she said, as she sat down, taking in the other guests. 'The couples here, all the women are, like, half as old as the men.'

I looked around and thought I'd noticed this too, but hadn't registered it. She ordered for us and while she talked about my book and the literary magazine she worked for I stared at her hands. I couldn't take my eyes off them. Her fingers were also tattooed, and adorned with gold rings and long pointed nails. It was the fashion, but all I could think of was Marguerite de Navarre; this was how I had imagined her hands when I read about them, minus the tattoos.

The journalist took out her phone and placed it in front of me on the table and, after pressing record, she asked me how I'd come to write a novel about breastfeeding and about taking care of a small child.

The question made me flinch. I'd been asked it so many times lately, and it was as if the shame I somehow felt writing about being a mother still had a grip on me. I explained that I hadn't wanted to, really: it was an impulse I had taken pains to suppress. Which was true. I did see it that way.

IN RETROSPECT, IT seems bizarre to have kept myself from writing what I wanted to most of all. At the same time this is a mechanism I've become well acquainted with. It wasn't actually specific to the subject of motherhood: somewhere deep down I'd always tried to stop myself from writing about what I felt a strong desire to and I wondered if this hadn't rendered every subject taboo for me. I had long understood that I wrote about what was taboo, not necessarily for society in general, but for me – but it could just as well have been the writing itself, the illicitness of it, that made everything it touched shameful and forbidden.

I had viewed motherhood as a cliché about womanhood that I wanted to distance myself from, but it was
also an experience that couldn't be overlooked and was
unlike anything else – the only thing that could compete
with writing.

I think it was after the interview when I left the hotel that
night that the story revealed itself to me fully, and I remember this making me feel even guiltier. Did everything about
women have to be about motherhood? I went to a Mexican
restaurant for tamales and tequila. It was hot and dark outside; at the tables around me people were talking about their
jobs and about making it in Los Angeles; the street was like
a black channel running along the outdoor patio and as I sat
there, taking it all in, I remembered the point with stories
about motherhood – they were equally about having once
been born as they were about giving birth. Yet again I had
forgotten this. I kept forgetting it. I still do. It's one of those
things I need to remind myself of, because I so seldom hear
anyone say it.

To some extent everything I wrote was about the body,
however much I resisted. So why was this so hard to accept?
My desire to do so was greater than the sense that I shouldn't,
the fear of nudging up against the feminine that came from
my aversion to biological determinism, male society's as well
as feminism's own, those who wanted to elevate women,
who wanted to believe in *woman* with a capital W as a figure

with particular characteristics and a particular goodness who should be rewarded with special treatment.

In my apparently always equally hopeless categorical way, I had associated stories of motherhood with stories of the virtuous feminine, with essentialism and difference feminism. I had come of age in a time when there was much discussion of the differences between women and men that arose because of nature or nurture and still could be seen as justification for a division in society where women were defined by what was specifically 'feminine' and didn't belong in the male arena. This conclusion provoked me so much that it seemed the only way to go was in the opposite direction and to fully suppress the biological, as though one extreme perspective could only be combated with another as extreme, or as though in the universe's quest for equilibrium only a polar stance could get the opposition to change their minds. This position might also have been what was needed then.

I don't want to belittle it, but when I look back and see how dominant this mode of thinking had been for me and those in my circle, I was dismayed that I hadn't noticed how I'd been as ideologically driven as I was accusing others of being, and how this had in turn hampered me as an author.

WHEN I WOKE, it wasn't morning yet but still night, but because I was going to fly home the same day, I made no effort to fall back to sleep. Instead I went straight from the bed to the desk and wrote for a couple of hours, before I packed my things and went out into the hall and rode the old creaky elevator down to the lobby and took a seat in the bar with my laptop.

Two white-clad waiters were busy setting up for breakfast. The older of the two served me tea in a large silver pot and asked, as he had often done over the past days, if the tea could be his treat. I nodded gratefully because it was an expensive tea and then I eavesdropped on his phone call with a vendor who, by the sound of it, was late with the morning delivery of baked goods. Once he'd hung up, he asked me what I thought of Los Angeles.

'You talk like a writer,' he said. 'What do you do?'

When I told him, as concisely as possible, he started talking about his son who was studying at UCLA and had recently started a year-long exchange in Europe, more specifically at the Sorbonne.

'Let me show you what got here yesterday,' he said, and took something out of a box in the bar. 'I'm not even going to try to pronounce it, but see.' He held up the card. 'It's the chateau our chateau was built after. That one's much bigger so it's not an exact copy but, yeah, you see? It's a sorta copy.'

I took the postcard, held it in my hand and looked at it.

Château d'Amboise.

I was speechless.

And so it was, this castle was the Chateau. Had I known but forgotten? Is this why I'd booked a room here?

The telephone at the bar started ringing and the bartender disappeared. A man came down in his stockinged feet and took a seat at a table and was served orange juice and two boiled eggs, apparently without having ordered them. He nodded to me. I returned his greeting and looked past him, out through the doors open onto the garden.

It wasn't really light yet, but I looked up at the grey walls and the morning between them, the windows with their hundreds of small leaded glass panes, the pinnacles and towers with pointed black roofs that looked exactly like the card in my hand.

I don't know what to write about the signs. I wonder if I can suggest anything about them at all without sounding like a loon. But does it matter how I appear? I want to say no, but maybe it's of vital importance for the rest of the story, and so for her. That my voice not contaminate it.

But it's probably too late for that.

I was seeing signs everywhere and I thought they were helping me. I clung to them. It was the little things and how they revealed themselves, the wider contexts I kept thinking I was seeing. They were recurring. From time to time I was filled with such deep gratitude for the universe's every remarkable gesture, which I couldn't help but interpret as an indication that the story belonged as much to me as to anyone else.

I was an author and I'd written several books. Yet I kept searching for excuses to be allowed to write. I'd thought it was a problem specific to this story but, deep down, I knew it had always been present in me. It resurfaces, whatever I do. Writing is accompanied by a constant sense of shame and guilt, in writing instead of working with something that could be of use to others, in living for writing instead of togetherness, in transforming other people's lives, taking all this reality and turning it into words, forcing it onto paper because . . . Yes, why?

I believed in the signs and I still believe in them. But I've repeatedly been made to see that there are logical explanations. Such is the passage of time. Kings and queens and captains make sure they are remembered after their lives are done, their actions echo through eternity just as they wished them to, their monuments are everywhere and everything we do is an after-effect of their movements.

Authors have their reasons for writing books, but for me it was as though no reason was good enough. Mine seemed unclear and insufficient. Were books but a way of processing what was hard or impossible to master? It strikes me now how this insight, as it relates to Marguerite de Navarre, unlocked her books for me and made them meaningful, whereas with my own books I would add that little word 'just' before saying what I was writing about, because my work felt so trivial. To think about writing was to think about my shortcomings and of how I'd *handled* my life so far; it filled me with self-loathing to remember how I had turned away from the living and written only for writing's sake, but above all how I turned every problem into words, like an animal who nourishes itself on its own excrement.

Writing was an addiction. I'd read this assertion on so many occasions but hadn't understood it until now. It implied a way out of every crisis, large and small, and it offered the illusion of an arm's length of distance whenever I encountered a hurdle, so I never needed to overcome it: all I had to do was get to the text. My existence had become dependent on the sharp white light that can rise up from one side, but also on the knowledge that I would never have to participate, that my existence wasn't subject to the same terrible conditions as everyone else's, because I would never need anyone else as long as I had my writing.

She'd been forced into isolation, but I had chosen mine. I'd sought it out in a way that tormented me later, after I'd become aware that was what I'd done. How I alienated myself from everything and everyone. I'd thought that writing this book was so hard because my friend had told me not to do it, and this probably would have been the easy way to see it. But as I moved through the dark months of the year, I realised that something else was threatening the writing, something I thought only pertained to me.

However, in reality, nothing pertained only to me. I belonged to everything around me and somewhere, deep down, I knew I might not have actually been as alone as I felt. I wasn't alone in experiencing the powerlessness I felt or in the dejected questioning of where all this was heading. I blamed the darkness when I couldn't write or read or sustain a thought, how it settled over me so quickly and shut everything off – but there was more to it, at least there was more to it than the darkness that was blacking out the sky. Winter had brought with it a cruelty that belonged to more than the dark and the cold, but which placed an equal strain on life. And my life was still my work, even if I had sensed what more was there, the blurred edges of which I could only imagine so far.

I'd long done everything I could to not treat being an author as an occupation that demanded special circumstances. I'd dismantled the rituals I'd become accustomed to and learned to write anywhere and anyhow. It was the very condition of my work, and my role as a parent. But now I was consumed with the question of where to find light, forever searching for places that were open enough and high enough or where the buildings were so low the sun could reach down to me from the sky. When I did find a moment to work in the daylight, it was enough to give me a glimpse of the ease I had previously felt.

I no longer went around waiting for inspiration and neither did I engage in marathon writing sessions while everything crumbled around me – but I needed the light.

Maybe I didn't need it to write, maybe I needed it to live, and living had become so intimately connected with writing. When it worked I felt good and when it didn't I felt dissatisfied. With everything. I complained to my husband and he said this was nothing out of the ordinary – I was like this whenever I was in an intense period of work. Naturally, I protested and, making no effort to hide my bitterness, replied that I wasn't in an intense period of work and that was the problem, but he persisted: I always felt like this, at least that's the impression I gave off. It was a well-meaning reminder, and on some level I knew he was right, but still I didn't want to hear it.

In the darkest time, the days all followed the same pattern. I fell asleep as soon as I lay down at night – it was more like being put to sleep than falling asleep – and every morning when I woke up, I turned over in bed so that I could look at the black sky peeking through the gap between our window and the old white blind, which was wrinkled and smudged with newspaper ink at the bottom. In those moments my only wish was for the darkness outside not to be anything but darkness, so the day would be clear. When the light did appear, on the days it did at all, I tried to get out of the apartment, but the problem was I'd also want to be working then. I read articles about how the lack of light here in the far north disrupts the circadian rhythm and encourages melatonin production, making you dopey and tired in the middle of the day. I had started using an anti-jetlag device I'd bought to help keep my trips shorter since I'd started feeling like I didn't want to be away from home for longer than necessary. It was a Finnish invention, with earbuds that shot light through the ear canal in order to stimulate the brain functions reliant on it. Every day before lunch I put them in my ears, even though I wasn't sure whether or not they worked. I read too about the symptoms of so-called seasonal affective disorder: an abnormal appetite, a great need for sleep, increased sensitivity, heaviness in the arms and legs.

'Those are all symptoms of a run-of-the-mill depression,' my husband said, when I listed them.

Regardless of the season, I preferred to work early in the mornings and before noon, but now it seemed impossible to get anything done later in the day. It was like an iron screen had been pulled down over me, further and further down until only a strip of air remained. I hunkered over sentences, and my every thought seemed to stem from impulses from the most primal parts of my mind, as though those were the only parts that were still functioning. I would often discover that I'd been staring at a single line for ages, moved one word, deleted another. Still I had questions. Writing demanded time and sometimes time had to be devoted to what was apparently unnecessary – had I let it go too far, or was what I was doing necessary?

When asked, I'd say it was going well, like I said it was going well with the kids and with everything else, as though I weren't the one speaking, but someone else inside me. I'd never considered myself to be a person who wanted to smooth over what wasn't good or easy, but something about parenthood had changed that. Maybe I said this as an incantation for myself, to avoid expressing what I actually felt because it frightened me.

The idea of no longer having access to writing terrified me. When I looked at the paragraphs of text in front of me, it felt as though I were on the outside looking in at something unmoving and dead. And I was the one who'd killed it, with

my compulsion and my inability to let go and move on. I
wasn't even sure of what I was writing.

I didn't know what and, above all, I didn't know why.

The psychologist I would go to had asked me what I was
avoiding thinking about by thinking about this project. I
didn't really offer an answer; presumably I had one, but I
don't think I dared come right out and say it.

I was a woman spending my days thinking about another
woman thinking about a man. It had become normal for me.
What did other people think about? I no longer knew.

I'm starting to picture Marguerite de Navarre more clearly as I read. The hand that holds the pen, the grey graphite tip, her long, sharpened nails. She looks so collected as she writes, quick and concentrated, and I think it's probably correct that she wrote the stories in *The Heptameron* for François I in order to cheer him up and help him on the road to betterment – but not for this reason alone.

In his 1935 book *Marguerite de Navarre,* the English literary critic Samuel Putnam called her 'the first modern woman'. This confused me. Hadn't I read that the first feminist was Christine de Pizan, who had been alive during the Middle Ages? What was the difference between a feminist and a modern woman? I was so unpractised in thinking about history – to me every word of the book of history had already been written – I had no understanding of how the past continues to stretch out behind us as we're observing it, and how the story is constantly being rewritten. Christine de Pizan, who herself wrote about how women had been erased from history, was only properly acknowledged during the 1900s, when Simone de Beauvoir and other academics started reading her. (I understand very

well that today there are many clear differences between 'feminists' and 'modern women', and I understand that the desire to
label women who lived before feminism as feminists or proto-
feminists can be irritating.)

Like Marguerite de Navarre, Pizan devoted much of her
time to Boccaccio, and she is also thought to be the first
woman who was able to support herself as an author. She
had started writing at twenty-five in order to support her
family after her parents had died. I'd think about this when I
felt incompetent and irresponsible for being an author. How
would I manage if I ended up alone, and what would happen
to my writing then?

I had turned to Pizan, as Navarre had, to find out her
thoughts about the island: things I was wondering but had
not been addressed by André Thevet and which I assumed
she never would have thought of telling him, even if she had
wanted to, like what she thought of the man without a name
and her reaction when she saw him on the boat – putting her
emotions into words. I also continued reading Louise Labé,
who was born in 1522 and may have been around her age; I
read Labé's love poems as though they contained a hidden
key, and I often returned to one of her epistles on reading
and writing:

Since a time has come, Mademoiselle, when the severe laws
of men no longer prevent women from applying themselves

to the sciences and other disciplines, it seems to me that
those of us who can should use this long-craved freedom
to study and to let men see how greatly they wronged us
when depriving us of its honour and advantages. And if any
woman becomes so proficient as to be able to write down
her thoughts, let her do so and not despise the honour, but
rather flaunt it instead of fine clothes, necklaces, and rings.
For these may be considered ours only by use, whereas the
honour of being educated is ours entirely.

So Labé had felt compelled to instruct other women on how to behave. But shouldn't they be able to tolerate it? And if women's views of themselves as ornaments was in the least bit problematic today – in spite of everything, I have to admit to occasionally seeing it this way too – what must it have been like 400 years ago?

I showed the epistle to my daughter and when, as usual, she asked my opinion – whether or not I agreed – I said I did and that the text was still relevant because it was a reminder of the value of knowledge, if not specifically for women.

I wondered if it was obvious or if it was one of those things that needed to be said, that as an adult I needed to say to her. There were a lot of things I had long avoided talking about, not just with her but in general, in every context, because I thought they were so self-evident they hardly needed mentioning, but something had changed.

I'd started noticing that what I had seen as a given wasn't anymore, and I suspected that the reason it had become like this may have been the very resistance I had been feeling – and which so many of my generation felt – about stating the obvious.

Christine de Pizan often turned up when I read about Marguerite de Navarre; Pizan who, in her book *The Book of the City of Ladies* from 1405, had described how she as a literate woman had been confronted with a history of male dominance and so had pointed out women's historic feats. She addressed God directly and asked him:

> *Didn't you yourself create women especially and then endow her with all the qualities that you wished her to have? How could you possibly have made a mistake in anything?*

It reminded me of how I had thought of him as a child. If God was perfect, why weren't women? Since he was the one who'd created everything? I googled *The Book of the City of Ladies* and found a series of miniature paintings from one of the editions of the book. One of them depicts Pizan kneeling before Isabeau, a French queen who'd often rule during her husband's spells of mental illness, and giving her one of her books.

Marguerite de Navarre had more than once been depicted similarly, presenting a book she had written to another woman, and it is a motif I recognised from my own life:

an image of consensus that could be either enticing or dis-
couraging. An image from the world of women. A universe
shared between two people of the same sex, between reading and writing, captured in a brief scene. It was the other
side of not counting, not belonging to the regular world but
to the world of women.

IN TALE LXVII, Marguerite de Navarre wrote of her that
she never wavered in her faith. I read it as an insinuation,
in two ways. First that Navarre had written 'her' faith; in
other words, the special and forbidden faith she had. Second,
Navarre suggests that she knows or has found out something
about Marguerite's life before the island. I frequently mulled
this over: how they came to know each other and whether
they had met afterwards, or that Marguerite de Navarre had
at least been aware of what happened after.

For a long time it seemed strange to me that Navarre
was so interested in religion. The descriptions of her as a
confused and indecisive debater were probably what led to
my lack of clarity over which side of the religious conflict
she was on. She was loyal to her brother and his fight for
Catholicism and she remained a member of the Catholic
Church her entire life, but she wrote about a personal faith
without sacrament and supported reformers, which has also
been interpreted as a sign that she followed the new faith.

Among those who Marguerite de Navarre gave asylum to at her court was the author François Rabelais, who dedicated the third book in his suite of novels about Pantagruel – often referred to as one of the most notable humanist literary works of the French Renaissance – to her. In the dedication Rabelais asks Marguerite de Navarre if she can imagine coming off her high horse (her 'eternal, heavenly place', he had written), to partake in the third part of Pantagruel's hilarities. Would the grand queen consider engaging with more earthly affairs if but for a moment?

His words to her were familiar. I had heard them so often, both figuratively and literally: a man asking a woman to take herself down a peg. Somehow an exalted woman was always seen as being a little more exalted than an equally exalted man; as though being exalted only became problematic when combined with womanhood. As though the presumed refinement in it made the woman more oblivious to the world, less human and more worthy of peoples' contempt – even though, no matter who she is and how much formal or informal power she has, she is simultaneously subordinated to men. When I read Rabelais's dedication I was reminded of the misogyny that runs through all time, shimmering and cursory but so strong that you lose your ability to think when it strikes.

Based on what I knew, I could only imagine that religion was viewed with a measure of scepticism by the intellectual women of the time. But then I read that the reason Navarre took an interest in questions of faith was because it was the only subject her brother didn't care about. She was more intelligent than he was and had the same education, thus she had to find an area in which she would never risk competing with and outshining him, hobbling his self-confidence. The problem was that he didn't remain uninvolved, or couldn't remain, so as the religious conflicts worsened. For her entire life she was loyal to him, even if it put her at great risk when his political interests contradicted her convictions.

Another reason why Marguerite de Navarre was so unremittingly devoted to God has been thought by many to be that she never found satisfaction in the relationships she had with the people around her. Previously I would probably have seen an assertion like this as coloured by hate, and would have asked myself why women in particular are assumed to be dependent on their relationships – but I don't think this way now. I consider what I read about all of her marriages being unhappy, all of the sons she gave birth to dying, and how her only daughter, Jeanne, who later also became queen and the leader of the French Huguenot movement, hated her because she had agreed to allow François I to marry her off when she was only twelve.

Now when I go through my notes about Marguerite de Navarre and the other two contemporary sources Thevet and Belleforest, I see how I was devoting myself to them in order to avoid doing what I really needed to do. It was in the middle of winter, and however hard I tried to keep making progress, I kept getting mired in the details. I did everything I could to stop myself from spending an entire afternoon on a single passage or article, hunching over the computer until the lines merged and I fell asleep out of pure exhaustion. So it was my usual problem, but not exclusively. There was also movement: I started to suspect that my subconscious was making sure I was entering new arenas so I didn't have to progress with the story. Instead of forwards, I went in other directions, digressions that led me to sidetracks that took me ever further away from the road I needed to stick to, and which allowed me to linger in thoughts of her as she was before everything started to fall apart, when it was still just all about her.

I spent a lot of time cleaning out my computer, because it made me feel like I was doing something, and due to my roving about every historical corner of the internet, I'd amassed a wealth of documents of which I didn't really have an overview.

One day, as I was sitting in our kitchen and reviewing files that were taking up a lot of space, I found a PDF with a long name that I didn't recognise: 6011-11477-1-PB. I opened it and saw eighteen densely typewritten pages that must have been scanned and uploaded to wherever I'd found them, which I'd saved to my computer only to then forget about them. A sentence on the first page caught my eye. It said something along the lines of: if Simone de Beauvoir saw the relationship between the sexes during the twentieth century as a relationship between aggressors and prey, then the same could be said about Marguerite de Navarre's era.

It had been written at the end of the 1900s, more precisely 1982, but the same could be said today. Thereafter came an account of how the women of the 1500s were entirely at the mercy of men, how they lived like their dogs, and the author stated that Marguerite de Navarre discussed this in her stories. The way men controlled women's destinies was a frequently recurring theme.

A snowstorm was forecast that day and, as I sat reading the document, snow gathered on the mullions of the kitchen window. The table was right by the window: I had moved it closer to get more light and, as I had, I'd been struck by how this action, the tabletop in my hands and me pushing the table across the floor until it touched the windowsill, clarified the hopelessness of my situation. I wondered if I was losing my mind, and if the question itself implied that this was the case. If you're doing the wondering, then maybe there's no question: you're losing your mind.

I looked at the PDF again and pictured the author, a young researcher in literature or gender studies with a slightly goth rock style. Black clothes, messy make-up, thick eyeliner. I copied the text to the Apple Books app so I could read it on my phone. I often read on my mobile and sometimes I thought this, in and of itself, could be part of the reason why I was having difficulty concentrating. I had shut off all notifications but reminders and pings still arrived, or maybe it was me who couldn't help but check Instagram or take care of a task in some app or answer an email. Though it was practical to be able to read while I waited for the children or was in line at the supermarket, which I often was because I was among those who still chose to pay at the till instead of at the self-checkout. Ages ago I would have loved an automated checkout system, but now I didn't feel the need to avoid standing in front of another person; on the contrary, I was happy to do it and to be able to say those brief standard phrases: 'hi', 'yes', 'yes, thank you', 'no, thank you' and 'thank you very much'. A recurring conversation devoid of content with people with whom, as far as I knew, I had nothing in common. Maybe it was because I spent so many hours of the day on my own, and now I was experiencing an utterly new solitariness on top of everything else. The great wave that had rolled through my existence had swept me closer to some but much further away from others. Sometimes I think it must be the irony of fate, how a new insularity rose in me right as I was trying to find my way out of the one I had created. I only have myself and my nearest and dearest now. It's probably never been any different, I just couldn't see it before.

WINTER ON THE island lasted from October to May. It was almost as dark as here, longer and much colder, with constant high winds from the north. On Cartier's first voyage to Canada he thought the cold season there would be similar to France because the latitude was the same, but in fact it was as cold as in Siberia. The lowest temperature on record in North America in modern times is -63 degrees Celsius, but back then it was even colder. The period in which she found herself there coincided with what has been called the Little Ice Age. It wasn't long after the pack ice in the North Atlantic had melted, and there were large areas where the permafrost never left the earth, and others where there wasn't any earth, only stone and chilled bedrock on which snow fell.

I moved more files to my laptop's bin and looked at images on a website for entertaining news that had popped up while I was searching for something else: *Thirteen images from Russia that will make you stop complaining about winter*. There were big rigs buried in thick snow up to the driver's seat; tall trees encased in ice; people in sleeping-bag-like coats, their breath in clouds around them; a man chiselling ice off his car with a hammer. I thought about the quiet chill on the island, and when the wind howled against the window, I looked out at the storm and imagined her looking out of the cave.

Even when the weather was mild I had a hard time tearing myself away from the computer and getting out of the apartment, but now it was a real struggle. Cutting it fine, I managed to get myself out into the snow and pick up the children from after-school care and take them to their sports. I sat on the bench with everyone else who tagged along, mostly babysitters or grandparents – not parents – and while I waited I pulled up the PDF in Apple Books.

The article described how Marguerite de Navarre's stories free the female characters from 'the thrall of mythic privilege', namely the image of women as temptresses and saints, and turn them into human beings of flesh and blood. I got to the last page and saw the author's name: Robert W. Bernard. So, a man had written it.

I googled him and at first I only found articles about plastic surgery and ads for a book called *Surgical Restoration of the Aging Face*, but then the right Robert W. Bernard appeared on the screen in my hand. I could tell it was him: a smiling man with thick glasses and a round face. Next to the picture it said that he had been born in 1935, had two children from his first marriage and as a 'devoted son' had lived with his mother in her final years. He'd discovered his great love for French literature at the University of Saint Thomas in Saint Paul, Minnesota, and later earned a PhD with his dissertation on Christine de Pizan.

Of course. But I'd barely finished my thought about how those two women always seemed to follow one another when I saw that the site I was on was called legacy.com. It was an obituary. Emptiness spread through me. Wasn't this always the way? I'd recently finished a book I'd bought over fifteen years ago, *Appetites: Why Women Want* by Caroline Knapp, which had long lain unread at home; I had taken off the dust jacket while I was reading it and, once I'd finished and was putting it back on so that I could reshelve it, I saw that Knapp had died shortly after it came out in the USA, not of the anorexia she discusses in the book but of breast cancer.

I was caught off guard by how sad this made me and I was as equally upset that Robert W. Bernard was no longer alive. I came to think of letters I had received and never answered, people I thought about calling but never called, and how short the remaining time might be, the time until I would be gone and someone who had just finished reading an old piece of my writing would google my name and find a few brief lines about who I had been and what I'd left behind.

In retrospect it seems so trifling. A passion like any other – a fire that ravages everything only to sputter and die out, be stifled by reality, with all its impossibility.

I write that she ends up sitting on the rock where they put her, right there, and from this spot she watches them climb back into the lifeboats and push off from the beach and start to row. The weapons, the round powder keg and the box of ship biscuits are at her feet. She holds her book loosely in one hand. The thin pages are wet with seawater, as are her shoes and clothes. Everything is wet. She hadn't seen him anywhere; she wonders why he didn't do anything, but also if this is an arrogant thought. What did she expect him to do?

Carefully she props the book up on the rock so that it can dry in the wind and then she looks across the strait at the fleet. She doesn't look at Damienne, who is pacing where the beach meets the forest, as though testing the terrain for a way out. She stops at the forest's edge and looks into the trees and seems to be listening for the animal noises described by Donnacona and his sons as the sound of a thousand men screaming simultaneously.

When I looked at pictures from the island it was hard to imagine where the animals would have hidden themselves. The forest looked so small, flat and sparse. Yet it contained the animals. Had they always lived there or had they, as Thevet wrote, come from all around, swimming or crossing over from the large forests on the mainland during winter when the ice in the bay was thick – and if this was the case, what had driven them there?

Damienne walks in among the trees and disappears, reappears. Her figure frees itself from the woods and she comes running back, a body unused to running. She bolts for the rocky beach where the demoiselle is sitting, as though she were being chased, hurls herself at one of those wet guns, picks it up and turns to face the forest but loses her grip, surprised by its weight.

Marguerite looks at her, then at the forest. There's nothing there.

For them the island is reality. It's not big and there's not much there. At first I thought maybe it hadn't been so bad after all; it may have been different for them than it would have been for me or someone else from my time – because their lives from the start were in all likelihood much more difficult than ours. But at the same time, everything became much worse for them. It must have done. Especially since they were already aware of the threat they were facing.

According to André Thevet in *La Cosmographie Universelle*, the arquebuses were at the ready from the first day, from the first moment. I thought Jean Alfonse might have convinced Roberval to arm them, either by talking him into it or in another way – by reminding him that a death sentence for fornication couldn't be reconciled with modernity, especially when it regarded such a young person who was also his ward. But the more I read about those weapons and how they were constructed, the clearer it became that they wouldn't necessarily make a difference. They were in no way a guarantee for survival but rather offered a sort of hypothetical opportunity to improve their odds for survival:

an arquebus required no fewer than twelve manoeuvres to load, and another three to shoot.

Thevet posited that of all the animals on the island the bears were the worst. It was overrun with them and at the time of their arrival, the females would have just given birth to their young. I had started following a *National Geographic* photographer on Instagram and on the same night, as I lay in bed looking at my phone before drifting off to sleep, a picture of a bear caught my attention. Its snout was narrow and long and its head had a special shape, not at all dissimilar to the drawing in *La Cosmographie Universelle*. In the caption the photographer described how he used camera-rigged traps to photograph animals in the wild. I looked through all of his photos because I wanted to see a picture of a wolverine, but there wasn't one.

A wolverine is a scavenger and omnivore common to many places in the world, but now endangered. According to Wikipedia, wolverines are not found around the Gulf of Saint Lawrence – the red fields marking the species' range start further north, near Ontario and the southern tip of the Hudson Bay. But they were there then.

My guess was that they terrified her.

I had hoped to see a wolverine at the Musée de la Chasse et de la Nature, a hunting museum which we also visited during our weekend in Paris. I told my daughter she had to come with me even though she didn't want to. I didn't actually want to involve her in my work but perhaps I'd felt like I should remind her that our trip was a business trip for me. There were certain things I needed to do while we were in France.

I thought what parents throughout time have thought: her upbringing was so different to mine. The thought had come with relief: I was glad to have managed to give her what I hadn't had, but the older she'd got, the more I noticed my impulse to inculcate certain essential things, such as a job like mine not being normal, such as nothing in life is free, no matter how it seems. I often chose the wrong occasion for these minor educational offensives. It was as though I couldn't allow her (and myself) to enjoy what was enjoyable: I constantly felt compelled to point out how grateful we should be for our privileged life. And each time I did I could feel how stupid it was.

The hunting museum was housed in two buildings from the 1700s on the corner of Rue des Archives and Rue des Quatre-Fils and had recently been renovated and reconceived, apparently to draw an art crowd and to take advantage of the contemporary predilection for taxidermy. The woman at the ticket desk spoke warmly of a Jeff Koons and a recently unveiled installation by a young Israeli artist in one of the new rooms on the ground floor. I listened and thanked her, but once we'd obtained our tickets, we went straight up the stairs to the permanent collection on the second floor.

It was like stepping into the private apartment of an eccentric old count whose favourite hobby was hunting. As soon as I walked into the first room, I saw a male polar bear standing on its hind legs, his paws reaching out in front of him, as though he were about to grab hold of something or someone to wrestle down and tear apart. It might not have been a male, but this is what I'm writing. His fur was white and surprisingly lustrous and fluffy, not the least bit yellow as I knew they could be, but rather it had a bluish tint. I wondered if it had been treated somehow to achieve that hue.

The sight of the bear had stopped my daughter in her tracks, but now she was walking right up to it. She was tall but only reached up to his chest, which made her look small. She stood on her tiptoes and reached for the polar bear's pale claws, almost nudging one. I fished my phone out of my pocket and took a picture, put it away again and glanced at the guard in the dark suit standing a few metres behind us.

He responded with a barely perceptible shrug.

My daughter turned to me. 'Are they really this big?' she asked.

'Apparently so,' I said. 'This one's real. It used to be alive.'

The look she gave me suggested this was a repulsive thing to point out to her. (Was it because it had once been alive or because it was now dead and standing here?) I wished I could sound more heartfelt when I spoke to her.

It was as though an unwelcome dullness would enter me, an arrogant tone or even disappointment, and I didn't know where it came from. As though my love for her was packed away inside me in something that became tight and impermeable. I thought about other mothers I know who always seemed to be able to make their love heard in their voices, no matter what they were saying. Other parents who seemed so good at getting their children to feel how much they loved them.

I took another picture. She made a face and got out of the way and I stood right in front of the polar bear and took one of it alone too. It looked unreal. It was the eyes. They were beady and made of round black glass, giving the face an almost comical quality. But then I remembered that was characteristic of polar bears, or at least a point of fascination for people: how their cuteness didn't align with their well-documented blood thirst.

My daughter had entered a dark corridor that led to the next room, and as I followed her, I glimpsed a brown bear inside, standing upright at full height, squeezed between two displays, about to attack or in mid-attack rather, looming over everything else in the room; its paws with their thick black claws and the wide-open mouth, its every sharp tooth visible.

'I thought they'd be smaller because I've never seen them standing up like this,' my daughter said.

I mm-ed in reply and thought that this was how they were depicted in the drawing in *La Cosmographie Universelle* too. They did indeed look much smaller there. Were the bears on the island smaller than these bears? I wished for them to be. The room wasn't particularly large but the ceiling was high. Along the walls were cases filled with hunting rifles, swords and bows and above them were shelves with stuffed animals of all kinds and in various sizes. But I didn't see a wolverine. In the middle of the narrow room was a row of glass cabinets, each containing numerous firearms from the last 300 years. Typical. What I kept finding was almost old enough but not quite. Seeing arquebuses from the 1600s or later wasn't good enough because so much about these weapons could have advanced in fifty, one hundred or one hundred and fifty years.

Then I saw a sign pointing to another weaponry room and I followed it. My daughter came after me. The room was dark with glossy floor-to-ceiling wood panelling and with even more glass cabinets along the walls. In a narrow window recess in one corner lay a catalogue with handwritten notes about the collection on display. Dotted around were drawings of small animals or objects, exquisitely rendered in fine, inked lines. I flipped through the substantial catalogue, page by page with an eye on the column for 'year' and photographed the pages where I found an item from the right period. The first was four crossbow bolts, which turned out to be right beside me. I only needed to

turn around to catch sight of them on a bed of black velvet at the bottom of a display case. She'd had a crossbow
on the island – Damienne had used it sometimes because
she was so afraid of the firearms they'd been given, but I'd
never thought about the bolts themselves. A streak of daylight from the window cut across them. They were simply made, their grey paint had flaked and the letters and
numbers that had been painted on the tips could barely be
discerned. It was hard to imagine that someone had used
them to kill an animal or even a person, pulling them out
and wiping them clean of blood when it was done. They
reminded me of the sort of mass-produced interior design
objects that had been popular for years and were meant
to look like weatherworn treasures from beaches in the
north-eastern United States.

I went back to the catalogue by the window. The week
before our trip I'd spent a lot of time in a forum where members with aliases such as Leprazy and Ghengis Khan discussed
the effectivity of old weapons – the longbow versus the first
firearm, for instance – and conducted long exchanges on
whether or not an arrow could penetrate armour, the types
of arrows and armours used during which epochs, and the
relative authenticity of historical reconstructions on various
TV programmes. The people in the forum were all men, or
at least presented themselves as such, and their posts shifted
between high-flown and colloquial, replete with spelling

mistakes and odd spacings between the words. A number
were chiefly concerned with choosing the correct gear for
some sort of role-playing game, while others wanted to daz-
zle with their posts. The tone they used with each other
was often snarky, if not to say flat-out hostile. All they could
agree on was that the early handgun compensated for what
it lacked in precision with its shock effect, especially in a
time when people didn't know how gunpowder worked
and still believed in spirits and magic. Especially on a desert
island, I thought, where nothing like it had been heard or
seen until then.

After browsing the catalogue for a while, I found that
the collection was meant to contain two arquebuses
of the sort she could be imagined to have had. When I
found the correct display I saw that they really weren't
so different to the newer models I had already seen. They
were at least two metres long, looked really heavy, and
the polished buttstocks were adorned with carvings and
small detailed images of angels, hunters and wild animals.
There they were, right in front of me, and I was struck by
how well preserved they were; but, on the whole, I didn't
feel anything in particular when I looked at them. What
had I hoped they'd impart? Suddenly I felt unsure of why
I'd even wanted to come here, and tried to bat away the
thought that I'd done all of this, the visit, the whole trip, to
avoid tackling what I actually needed to be doing.

My daughter appeared by my side. 'Almost done?' she asked. 'Are you finding what you came for?'

I didn't know what to say so I said nothing. She shrugged and sat down in one of the large velvet sofas in the next room. I cast a final glance at the old guns and gave a thought to those who had executed the ingenious decorative work, before I followed after her.

This room was bathed in half-light and except for a guard by one of the doors, no one was in there. I went up to a tapestry like the one I imagined François I to have brought with him when he arrived with his entourage at Château de Roberval to hunt. To my delight I noted that it was from the early 1500s. It could have been his. It could have been present at all of his parties. The many thousands of wool and silk stitches creating the enormous weave gave it a palpable lustre. The colours were faded but well-enough preserved for the motif to be discernible. It depicted a scene from the legend of Actaeon and Diana, an ancient myth that explores the boundary between the human and animal that was popular when humanism started to break through in Europe. During a red deer hunt, Actaeon loses himself in his desire for the goddess Diana and surprises her as she bathes, whereupon she turns him into a stag, who is soon devoured by his own hunting dogs.

This was basically how it was summarised on the sign next to the thick fabric. It covered the wall from floor to ceiling. The four dogs in the foreground were so sensitively rendered, while the man in his grand hunting garb had turned his large stag head, as if in surprise, towards the beautiful naked goddess and the women surrounding her. I couldn't get my fill of it: the refined textile art, but also the refinement of the revenge itself, transforming the hunter into the hunted.

When I noticed that my daughter had left the sofa and was standing behind me again, I thought, *That's enough now.* I put my arm around her and kissed her cheek, which was cool and soft, and we left the room and walked back down the stairs. She danced a few steps as she crossed the courtyard leading to the exit.

I followed her and wondered how heavy the arquebuses were and what they would feel like in my hands. I should have asked to hold one. Why hadn't I? I couldn't get over having not been able to ask for such a simple thing. But then I realised it would probably require special permission, which I didn't have time to secure.

I stopped for a while under the cool, dark archway leading to the street and I thought of her. I had wanted to see the weapons she had used and the animals she had fought, to form an image of all the things that could offer me some explanation; but, now that I had, it seemed even more incomprehensible.

I considered going back in and asking – maybe the friendly woman at the ticket desk could help me. But through the open door I saw my daughter standing in the sun, waiting for me. She was leaning against a lamppost and appeared to be looking down the street, and I was reminded of everything she wanted to do while we were here.

I write that they sit in silence beside each other on the beach, each holding a gun, looking between the archipelago, where the fleet is still visible at the far end of the inlet, and the forest edge where a beast could reveal itself at any moment. What they should do is not a given. There is no next step. They only know that they've been exiled, and it's as though it doesn't sink in until they've sat there for so long that they can see the ships really are sailing away, back out into the gulf.

The ocean is grey and the wind whips up high waves. A yellowish foam has accumulated on the beach and its peaks are clipped by the wind. She has never seen anything like it and that's probably why she's staring, as well as to avoid looking at Damienne, of course. When she finally looks up she notices another movement. Damienne hasn't seen it even though she's looking; the old woman's eyes haven't fared well with age.

But to her it's clear: there's something out there. She gets up, as though it would help her see, and stands there blinking at what seems to be approaching the island, trying to sharpen

her gaze. The lifeboat again. Only one person seems to be row-
ing this time. She takes her book from the rock and clutches it
as if hoping it might help, as though it could change his mind
and send him back there to fetch them. But then why are the
ships sailing in the other direction? The small vessel is heavy
in the water, bobbing in the waves. She soon sees that it's getting closer and whatever is happening, it isn't one of the men
returning: it really is just one man at the oars and he is larger
than they are. Is it him? It looks like him. Her knuckles whiten
around the book. Damienne joins her in standing.

The lifeboat containing the man without a name gets closer,
but he misjudges the depth and jumps out before the boat
has reached the shallows, his head disappearing underwater.
Then he pops up again. He keeps one hand on the gunwale.
He comes closer and closer and drags the boat, full of supplies,
ashore, and drops everything when he catches sight of her.

They go to each other. Damienne stands still, sits down
and averts her eyes as she runs to him and they embrace.
When they walk towards her, she gets up and walks away,
saying it's all her fault, she should have stopped them, it
was her job. She had one job. She roves around the rocks
wringing her hands as they stand there, holding each other.

THE SOURCES OFFER competing accounts of the disembark-
ment. François de Belleforest wrote that the captain left

his sister on one island – for in his book she is Roberval's
sister – and the man without a name on another, and that
he swam to her in order to save her. André Thevet states
that the man, probably wielding a weapon, seized more
supplies and gunpowder and weapons from the ship, and
loaded up the lifeboat with all of it plus his own arquebus,
sword, flintlock pistol and crossbow, and 'several bushels of
biscuits, his cithern, canvas, tools, and several other things
necessary for their service'.

But in Marguerite de Navarre's story the roles are
reversed. It is the man who is to be punished by the captain – he is a craftsman who was 'a most wicked man,
who betrayed his master and put him in danger of being
captured by the indigenous people' – and it is the young
'wife' who saves his life. When Captain Roberval –
she wrote the name but spelled it with a 't', *Robertval* –
is about to hang him, the wife intervenes: she who had
'followed her husband through the perils of the deep and
would not now leave him to die,' begs and prays for his
life. The captain answers her prayers – 'for pity of her
and for the sake of the services she had done them' – and
instead of killing him leaves them both on the island, and
allows them to bring a few useful items.

Damienne doesn't feature in any of the stories, but in what
André Thevet wrote, which lays claim to fact rather than fiction, it is clear that she was present. I assumed this detail

ruined the romance for the other authors. I might also have
omitted her, had I been able to.

When I read *A Colony of One* I thought about how much
importance Elizabeth Boyer placed on the question of
how the man arrived at the island – not just why and how,
whether he took a hostage or threatened to blow up the ship
with gunpowder or if he convinced Roberval, but in exactly
which way he did: if he swam ashore or arrived by boat or
waded or jumped from the large ship – and it calmed me that
not even Boyer, who seemed to have read and considered
everything, could be sure.

It did seem more likely that the man, who as far as she
could tell was a military man, would have taken a lifeboat
rather than throw himself overboard and swim to the island,
but it was also strange that Thevet doesn't bring up the lifeboat on the island again – how they used it. Maybe he forced
a man along with him who took the boat back to the ship;
maybe he took it alone but didn't pull it far enough up onto
the shore, so it was drawn out to sea by the current; perhaps
the boat has simply been left out of these stories. Seafaring
wasn't yet as established in people's minds. Heading out to
sea wasn't commonplace – not even André Thevet had been
anywhere; for years he had only heard eye-witness accounts
of the far-off places he was writing about. Only years after
his interview with Marguerite was he able, with support
from the Cardinal of Lorraine, to take research trips to Asia,

Greece, Rhodes, Palestine, Egypt and Brazil. But when he met her he hadn't been anywhere yet.

I recognised this feeling: writing about everything, but not being involved. Drawing maps, but not putting them to use.

The practical questions about how it had happened probably wouldn't have been impossible to answer if one were so inclined, but the other questions were still dogging me. Such as the one about what she actually thought of him. They had slept together on the ship, it had caused a scandal; *she* had caused the scandal by yielding to sin and to him. Was this love? As André Thevet proposes, it's easy to think that she did love him, but is that because he wanted to make it all worth her while or because she wanted it – or did she really? Was he a person she wanted to be alone with on a desert island and could a woman back then even have arrived at such a conclusion about a man, or did she just have to grin and bear it?

I saw the second picture one morning as I sat in the kitchen reading an English translation of *The Heptameron* on the computer while the children lounged on the living-room sofa watching *The Amazing World of Gumball* on the Cartoon Network. The animated characters' shrill voices rang through the rooms, as did the children's yearning commentary on the ads interrupting the show every ten minutes. What they wanted most of all was some sort of slime that could be stretched to one hundred times its size – and I could hear myself in their voices, in how the joy vanished from them, when they started telling each other that there was no way, these things never work like they do in the commercials.

The caption under the black-and-white picture read: *The Wife Reading to Her Husband on the Desert Island*. I stared at the screen. It was them. And behind them was the hut; well, it looks more like a hut than a log cabin. There was the palm tree again, or rather palm leaf; the persistent notion that there were palm trees in Newfoundland and Labrador. This was a new image of her, one I hadn't yet seen and hadn't known about, but most of all it was a picture of him. He is on the ground leaning against the hut and holding a cross in one hand and looking up at her. His face is round and swollen, his eyes protruding and his features somehow lumped together. He looks old. This wasn't at all how I'd imagined him. His gaze is on her and she is sitting over him, reading from a book. It's not as small as her chignon Bible but it could have been the same book – it's the only book named in the manuscript. Had the artist enlarged the book to show that she wasn't hiding the New Testament from him? Or had she taken several books with her; might she have been reading him Labé or Pizan?

It was still dark outside and the wind was blowing so hard you could hear it against the window panes. I felt disappointed. Hadn't I read that he was good looking? Or just that he was big and tall? He certainly was in this illustration. Next to him were items that matched Thevet's description of the supplies he'd taken from the ship: a gun, a sword and a few containers. He was properly dressed, as was she. She was wearing a high-necked dress and he was in a waistcoat and jacket, shirt and long trousers. But the picture looked to be much more recently drawn than the sixteenth century.

I made coffee and read the first three short stories in the book. When my husband got up and came into the kitchen, I showed him the picture. A mild giddy rush moved through me – it had to be the coffee – and that's probably what made me want to do it, share some of this with him. This is what

happened sometimes – then he might say something encour-
aging, which I thought sounded stupid and made what I was
showing him seem insignificant. He could take a paper from
a pile and read a few sentences aloud and comment keenly,
maybe even enthusiastically, on all that was great about what
I'd written and I'd immediately feel angry. How stupid of me
to think that it might be good – it was worthless! On the other
hand, if he didn't react positively enough, I'd have been even
angrier. As he leaned over me and studied the picture on the
screen, he pointed out that she looked almost identical to the
other picture. I looked at him. I hadn't seen it. Me, who saw
everything, how could I have missed this? And he who wasn't
particularly observant. This is what I was thinking.

I took out *La Cosmographie Universelle* and immediately saw
that he was right. The avian features, eyes set close together
with heavy lids. What did it mean? Had it been drawn by
someone who knew her face, or someone who had looked
at Thevet's illustration? Was this the aesthetic ideal for a
woman of her time? I looked up other pictures of women
in *The Heptameron* but none of them had the same bird eyes.

As with the illustration in the *La Cosmographie Universelle*,
this one was so different to my own idea of her. When I saw
her in front of me, her long hair was snarled and dirty, like
my own could be when I didn't think I had time for things
like washing my hair, and her face was hard and shadowy.
But this new picture made me wonder about something

else. It made me think that, upon realising he was the one in the lifeboat, she might not have been caught up in a swell of joy. Equally, he could have been persistent – they'd not slept together but he'd had designs on it, so he'd chased after her and Damienne to the desert island, and she cursed her actions even more when he turned up.

I had no trouble at all imagining this, so why had I been so sure that she was happy to see him, that the sight of him in the boat mitigated much of what else she was feeling? There was a script, of course, for how to interpret it all. But there was also the matter of them needing him there on the island.

I went on to the next story. Tale IV was one of the auto-biographical stories Marguerite de Navarre wrote based on her own experiences. It described an event in her life that I'd read about, unaware that she'd written about it herself, that this was how it had become known. Navarre, who was the most powerful woman in France, queen and both a prince and princess again – had on one occasion been subjected to an attack by Guillaume Gouffier de Bonnivet, one of France's top admirals, who was part of the circle of childhood friends with whom she and her brother had studied. After a party, when she'd retired for the night, Bonnivet had entered her bedchamber through a secret door:

Forthwith, having no regard for the duty that he owed his mistress or for the house to which she belonged, he got into

bed with her, without entreating her permission or making
any kind of ceremony. She felt him in her arms before she
knew that he had entered the room; but being strong, she
freed herself from his grasp . . .

Marguerite de Navarre's alter ego in the story defends herself
with fist and fingernail, and considering how close she was
to her brother perhaps she didn't hesitate to tell him what
happened, in spite of her lost honour, or perhaps the scratches
on her attacker's face brought it to light, but this matters less:
the interesting part is that the king did not reprimand him
in any way. He must have thought that this was the kind of
thing that happens. As I stumble upon Bonnivet's name on
the internet, now I see that in some places he is called a flirt
and a ladies' man.

Tale IV made me see how much my way of thinking about
this was suffused with the view of sex as an expression of love
and vitality. Even though I had always been surrounded by
stories concerning men's violence against women, I hadn't
even nudged up against the possibility that the man without a
name could have raped her on the boat, and might have come
after her on the island to do it again. The idea of sexuality as a
source of pleasure had started to emerge at this time – it was
one of the new modes of thinking with which Marguerite de
Navarre occupied herself, but rape was still seen as a method
of seduction. The degree of a woman's potential arousal

was what differentiated rape and intercourse. This view was clearly present even when I was growing up, and still I hadn't considered it in this context. I'd assumed that it hardly could have been the case because of her family ties to Jean-François de la Rocque Roberval. The works I had read about how he had loved her and sacrificed himself for her had made me disregard other likely scenarios, along with what I knew of how gender cut through every hierarchy and how a woman's social rank could never shield her from a man.

The autobiographical story reminded me of this but also that it doesn't matter how superior or strong a woman is in and of herself because she, whatever she does, can still be dominated by a man – by his emotions, his actions, his shortcomings, his weaknesses and wishes to expand. Marguerite de Navarre was a woman who had influence over the development of society at large, as well as over her own and others' lives, yet she was entirely dependent on her brother and the men she had to endure in order to keep her position.

The opposite view could also be taken. She was a woman who was forced to subordinate herself but who also challenged male power, through the power of her position but also her writing. Accounts of men suddenly popping up in women's beds were common in the literature of the age, but what was distinct – and innovative – in Navarre's stories, was that the women defended themselves and protested.

It didn't seem likely that the man without a name would have forced himself on her. It was probably more likely that what they had was love, I reasoned, but what did I know of love's meaning? It is hard to know what the word encompasses today, to say nothing of back then. There was something clichéd in how I was looking at their relationship – was it because of the centuries that lay between us, infusing the stories of that time with distance and romance? I spent a lot of time wondering how they viewed love and what they thought it could hold, but it was a while before I started to see that I should turn the question on myself instead. I was the one who still wasn't really getting it, who still had an idea of what it was to love that did not apply here.

I now think that she did love him, because I don't think Marguerite de Navarre would have called the love they had 'well worthy of praise' if she didn't have reason to believe it to be so; if she hadn't wanted to assert to the reader that this is what they'd shared.

It is only in his lesser known work on North America, the collection of documents titled *Le Grand Insulaire*, that André Thevet calls the man without a name her husband, but in their novellas both Marguerite de Navarre and François de Belleforest mention their marriage more than once. The first few times I read this, I took it as a romantic interpretation. I thought of the novels about her that I hadn't read, in which a marriage on the beach had surely been featured – but the other implications of the question of their marital status hadn't struck me. Followers of the New Testament could marry without an officiant, in a ceremony where a knot was tied instead of rings being exchanged, and even if no one other than Belleforest spells it out, this must be what they had done, because if they hadn't been married, she couldn't have told Thevet or anyone else about what happened later.

I came to wonder if the man without a name was also Protestant and if so, how this had come to light. Jean-François de la Rocque de Roberval's job was to spread Catholicism as the one true faith, so it is reasonable to think that during the crossing she must have continued to hide her faith. This couldn't have been a big deal if Roberval was doing the same thing (which I wasn't sure he was, after reading Thevet's description of him as tyrannical on account of his religion), but I wondered if she revealed herself to the man when they arrived on the island – or if it hadn't mattered. She could have just as well kept the precise meaning of her faith to herself because it belonged to her inner life, or that one of the time's biggest battles didn't really mean anything after all if you were on a desert island thousands of miles from home, where God became more important than ever. On one hand, she might not have paired up with him if he hadn't been Protestant; on the other, it wasn't anything he could have been public about. Or did her faith in God only emerge afterwards, when everything was over?

If it was true that she was Jean-François de la Rocque de Roberval's closest confidant, she must have, wherever she otherwise placed her faith, believed that he would return. She probably wasn't thinking, on those first days on the island, that he intended for her to die there. Of course it may have dawned on her later, but she could just as well have thought his reason for not returning was that the ship had been wrecked or that they had gone ashore by the river and been attacked by 'savages' and that he was dead. I wondered what the man without a name thought and how they discussed it; if he and Damienne may have understood the situation long before she did, and hid their thoughts from her.

I often thought about the man's arrival on the island in terms of salvation, but with him also came temptation, the risk of sin and being punished again. I swing between idealising the marriage and seeing it as a panic measure, an act they had to perform at once so as to not be punished by God, in one of the many ways he would be able to mete out punishment in this situation. To continue meting out punishment.

They must have realised that they were going to stay there, that nobody was coming to get them. They would be

living there together for an unspecified amount of time, trying to survive. I thought about the map of the island with
the half-naked white people standing between the angels and
devils, and turning away from them.

The first thing he does is set up the tent cloth so they can seek shelter from the wind. When evening arrives, they lie in the tent, the three of them, listening for sounds from the forest. But their first night passes in silence. Damienne lies between them, and when they hear that she is asleep, they crawl out of the makeshift tent and only when they are lying outside, at a slight distance, does it become perfectly clear to them that its protection is insufficient.

Thevet wrote that she calls the structure he begins to build the next morning a *logette*, a log cabin. When I read that, I thought it had an unexpectedly cosy ring to it – imagine them being able to build their own little cabin! I was as surprised at this as I was over how well-groomed she appeared in the illustration. In my sources it is mentioned that she helped him; they must have set to work right away, as soon as it was light, their weapons close to hand: the arquebuses, the sword and the crossbow that was Damienne's weapon of choice.

Elizabeth Boyer wrote with such devotion about the building in *A Colony of One*. Perhaps, like I, she found it almost incomprehensible that they had managed to construct anything at all, thinking about the place and its conditions, that they started felling trees and shaping them into timber logs instead of just lying down on the rocks and awaiting the beasts and the night. Her theories about the man's construction work go into as much detail as those addressing the conditions of his arrival on the island. She describes how he must have struggled to fell the trees and strip them of their branches, drag the logs across and raise them. He had taken several tools from the ship; I think they look out of place there on the rocks or leaning against a root on the ground, gleaming like the sharp marks of a far away civilisation. Marguerite and Damienne beg him to rest, but he persists. He raises walls and builds a roof. Makes a door with a bolt on the inside. Makes beds, which the women line with twigs and moss.

Perhaps it was also that Boyer, unlike me, had actually been to the island. She wrote that its square shape in the drawing in *La Cosmographie Universelle* matches what it looks like in reality and that everything is there, if depicted in a painterly way: the stream dividing the island to the north, the craggy outcrops, the indented coastline and how you can make out the surrounding islands. She also wrote that the flower-shaped object in the lower part of the picture is a type of shield, which she calls a *pavesse*. A battle shield from the Middle Ages. The man's shield.

When I look at them now it's obvious. How could I not have seen it myself?

Up on the left is a figure that is almost impossible to make out if you don't know it's there or if you don't take the time to scrutinise the picture. It is a tiny stick man on the island's north-western corner, who is moving away and carrying something on his back. A rifle or a cudgel maybe. It reminded me of a rune, simplified marks that don't correspond to the drawing as a whole, and like everyone else who has seen it I wondered who it was supposed to depict and where the person was going. But looking at it now, I can see it resembles my very first image of her. I also see the bears in the foreground differently. One is coming towards her and the other, who is lying on the ground, has already been shot. It took me months to see it, that one of the bears was already dead, but now it is so clear to me. When I look at the undulating form above her and above them, I can tell it represents a cloud of gun smoke rising from her weapon. I see the round hole high up on the bear's shoulder.

Thevet wrote that they killed a great many animals while on the island, and ate them. Navarre wrote in Tale LXVII:

> . . . *when the lions and other animals came near to devour them, the husband with his arquebuss and she with stones made so stout a defence that not only were the beasts afraid to approach, but often some were slain that were very good for food.*

Of course there were no lions on the island, but as with the palm tree, so with the lions; they were what was thought to have existed in the New World. According to a footnote in the translation of *The Heptameron* I have with me now, Navarre may have been confused, that what those who had visited Canada had spoken of were sea lions, not lions. And maybe she really did use stones at first and learned to use the arquebuses and the flintlock pistol later, but it's even more likely that she could already shoot. It's not hard to picture how this could have happened. If they had indeed met during one of the royal hunts in Roberval (one of those hunts where François I arrived with at least two of those three carriages, and his full hunting party of 300 men with as many horses, twenty hunting dogs and the fine porcelain dinnerware and tapestries and his entire court), he may have taught her then. I could see him standing behind her, holding the heavy arquebus as she loaded and lit it. They would have had to stand close, completely still.

A gun could so easily fire of its own accord or a shot could fly in the wrong direction.

My ideas about the high- and low-brow of writing weren't the only reason I'd ignored the role motherhood played in this story too. She became pregnant almost right away, or was already when she arrived on the island. It's how we know she married the man without a name, even though Thevet doesn't mention it, either in secret on the ship as in François de Belleforest's 'Third Tale' or on the island with Damienne as witness. She never would have told Thevet or anyone else about the pregnancy had they not been married.

In the 'Third Tale' she's already with child on the ship; according to Thevet's account it had happened in July 1542, which is to say once they had been on the island a while.

I had to take my fingers off the keyboard, I couldn't calculate it without using them – which intensified my feeling that I was losing my mind – but it was theoretically possible that they hadn't slept together on the ship, that she wasn't being punished for intercourse, but something else. What that was, I didn't know. I had googled 'sex in the 1500s' countless times without finding much that helped me understand what it could have been: which aspects of my images of the erotic belonged to my time, and which were eternal.

But with time the particulars leading to her pregnancy had come to mean less to me. I probably also realised that it couldn't have meant much to Roberval. He wanted to be rid of her and he wanted to avoid her bringing shame upon the fleet with her salacity, whether it had been real or if he had fabricated it so as to have an excuse. She might never even have seen the man without a name, never harboured a single feeling for him. Jean-François de la Rocque de Roberval may have thrust them together in order to have a reason to carry out his planned punishment. He may have had it in mind long before they set off from La Rochelle, perhaps since he first had heard about her father's passing and the road being clear for him to take her on as his charge.

It could also be that François de Belleforest had found out the truth from someone on board the ship, and that she had told André Thevet a different story. But if Belleforest's story was in line with reality, she would have already been pregnant when she climbed aboard the ship, because the child in his version is born after only six weeks on the island. If this was the case, had she wanted to protect him in her interview with Thevet, and so had made it sound as if she'd first met him during the crossing?

In a way it was remarkable that from one day to the next what had constituted such a large part of my thoughts about her stopped being important. My curiosity had turned to the birth of the child, rather than its conception. Perhaps it had to do with my sister-in-law asking if I wanted to be present for the birth of her son. Single women in Sweden had quite recently been given the legal right to have children via insemination or IVF, and in the public debate, misgivings were being aired about men becoming superfluous if women could reproduce on their own. When it came to people I knew going down this route, I'd found myself idealising their parenthood, seeing it as a symbol of freedom from conflict, and of courage. Now the thought of the child that was to be born made me feel even closer to her there on the island. What had she known about how it was growing inside her? Had she seen Leonardo's studies, might she have had the chance to look at them when she visited Amboise, were they in his studio there? Earlier theories were based on the Greek physician Claudius Galenus's image of the uterus as an inverted penis, which due to the weakness of the female sex hadn't been able to grow out of the body. Because women's bodies generally weren't available for autopsy, this description remained until 1511, when Leonardo da Vinci encountered a pregnant woman's corpse, cut open her abdomen and saw the position of the fetus inside.

As for me, I prepared myself by listening to lectures on what a companion could do during a birth and by watching videos that women had uploaded to YouTube. I lay with my

phone in my hand before bedtime and stared at the rock-
ing bodies and the transformation they seemed to be going
through from the first frame to the last. Their swollen faces,
eyes heavy, gazes turned inward, towards something spreading inside them, concentrating all their energy around it. The
pure fear in some of them, before they let go and gave into
the pain. But what I actually wanted to see – their child tearing them open from the inside and pushing out of them – was
edited away or covered with some sticker.

Thevet wrote that she started to grow as her husband
began to wither. I imagined him getting weaker with each
passing day on the island, whereas she grew stronger, in spite
of, or because of, the pregnancy. Also belonging to my idea
of the course of events was that the man was a sort of hero
to begin with, and I often thought about how she perceived
him once her wishes for what he could be to her had expired.

Her body expands in size as his shrinks. He can't build,
can hardly speak or eat. Because he's too heavy to move
out of the log cabin, she offers him a pail for his needs,
which she empties outside after each use. When his head-
aches intensify, she caresses his temples, and when his
whole body starts to itch, she tries to cool his skin and
bathe the scratches he inflicts on himself, removing the
skin and blood collected under his nails. She fetches him
meat, which she pre-chews, and water that she holds to his
mouth so he can take small sips.

What is it that allows her and Damienne to outlive him? Did they give him more to drink than they gave to themselves, because they thought the water they did not know was unclean would restore his health – or was he simply less hardy? I wonder if it would have been possible to offer a diagnosis today, or if a medical expert could point to a specific cause. Elizabeth Boyer seems to think it's the house-building that saps his energy. André Thevet offers another explanation. He wrote that the man fell sick with sorrow because, in their eight months on the island, not one ship had sailed by that could have rescued them and taken them back home. But is it possible to fall so ill with disappointment, from no one seeing your need and coming to your rescue? Surely it must have been a combination of factors. He could have hurt himself on a log or a tool or have been wounded by the unpredictable firearms during one of their first days.

She lies next to him on the first nights, careful not to make anything worse, and I assume she's already speculating about what might happen. At night, when he's half-awake and sweating and whispering disjointedly, long gasping sentences about things that are incomprehensible to her, does it frighten her and make her embarrassed for him, make her wish Damienne wasn't there to hear it, hoping she wouldn't wake up?

If he stays inside the hut during the day, she doesn't have to worry about accidentally shooting him with the arquebus, but handling the gun by herself presents its own challenge. She has to learn to aim at a long distance and preferably also hit her mark on the first try so as not to give her prey a chance to attack. Damienne is at her side with the charger and the powder keg, surveying the forest. Through the trees they move in pace; they take shifts sitting in a clearing; they try to find wolverines and lure the stags that traverse the grass between the forest's edge and the stream. The shot from their weapon sends the birds flying from the trees and hares dashing across the tracts. They down a hare in motion, carry it across the island, flay and slaughter it, prepare the meat over the fire and feed him small bites. In the beginning they had biscuits from the ship and, when they ran out, there was fruit, according to Thevet, and edible herbs, according to Navarre. She wrote that this sustained them for a time, but in the long run the man could not endure the diet – and they drank bad water.

When I first read that, the question of water hadn't yet come to mind. There were several fresh-water sources on the island. It was Jean Alfonse who on Jean-François de la Rocque de Roberval's orders had charted the fleet's route through the archipelago east of the river mouth in the northern part of the estuary, and when they sailed between the islands, I imagined that he'd made sure Roberval had chosen Île Sainte Marthe for her exile because it would be possible for her to survive there, at least for a while: a theoretical possibility if nothing else. It was large and hilly enough for there to be watering holes at an altitude that prevented them from being ruined by the salty waves that rinsed over the islands when it stormed. And yet, somehow, the water went bad while they were there.

They could have also found other food. Elizabeth Boyer seems to think Damienne worked a plot of land somewhere on the island, growing radishes and turnips and perhaps other vegetables, too, from seeds she'd taken from the boat.

Roberval didn't place much importance on this, and neither have I, but cultivating the land was a central part of their colonial project. In his writings, Jean Alfonse de Saintonge made many observations about soil quality and arability and stressed the importance of arriving in the new country in time to sow and thus harvest before the winter to avoid famine. Boyer wrote about the berries that could have grown there, blueberries and cloudberries, and about the wild bird eggs Damienne may have gathered for omelettes (being in possession of a frying pan seems even odder than him having tools). From the early explorers' testimonies, she wrote, it can be concluded that there were grey partridges, grouse and ptarmigans in the area, and the game birds are said to have been so tame that they could pluck the eggs right from their nests.

Upon reading this, I went straight to my youngest child's room to look for a book that was somewhere in the disarray.

The room had originally been built as a maid's chamber, set behind the kitchen with only enough space for a bunk bed and a bookshelf along one of the short ends. I searched through the shelf, finally found the book that played animal sounds and sat down with it on the floor, which was full of toys that I had to push out of the way in order to have enough space to open it up in front of me. They had been given this book one Christmas when they were little and used to pore over it. I was under the impression that my son liked the sound of a certain orangutan most of all, and that both of them used to express their disappointment with the big cats, whose sounds weren't the monstrous roars they'd expected but rather a soft cooing that was almost bird-like.

I found the ptarmigan and pushed the button on the small plastic speaker on the outside of the book. Nothing happened. I got up, walked through the kitchen to the broom closet and pulled out the toolbox, which I'd cleaned and organised a few days before when I was having trouble working. I found the smallest screwdriver, took it to the children's room and unscrewed the speaker's battery casing. It was empty. I went back to the broom closet and took out our box of spare batteries, but saw at once that they were all the wrong size. My son must have taken them out and stuck them in one of the robots he and his sister preferred playing with now. It didn't matter, I could have searched for the bird's call on the internet, but instead of going to the computer I went back into the children's room and immediately spotted the remote for one of the robots.

I put the remote's batteries in the book and then lay down in the lower bunk where my daughter slept. It bothered me a bit that she was on the bottom and he on top, but I'd let it be. I heard a slight snap in one of the slats when I squeezed in among her soft toys in that little bed; my youngest daughter was the first of my three children who really liked them and wanted lots, and I liked that. I liked buying them and I liked the sensation of my head on her pillow and the large book resting on my chest while a fluffy owl stared at me, its large eyes shining.

I pushed the button on the plastic speaker, flipped through the pages, pressed it again, and remembered what the children's fingers had looked like when they pushed it, how their faces had lit up when the sounds came, how their bodies felt in my arms when they were small.

I listened to the wolverine in the book and to wolverine sounds on a 'Creepiest sounds made by animals' clip on YouTube. As I listened, I understood André Thevet's many mentions of animals as representations of evil spirits on the island. It was almost impossible to imagine that animals could sound so terrifying.

I write that she's in bed in the hut when she hears it. The last thing the man had completed as part of the construction was the bolt on the door intended to protect them from the animals, but in this case it wouldn't be of any help. The wolverine must have been nearby, enticed by the smell of human bodies. She hears its claws rasping the logs, gets up and cracks the door open, but sees nothing. She goes back to bed only to be reawakened by more rasping as the wolverine digs away at the earth under the logs. In a flash, it's in the hut, charging through the dark, unleashing its eerie snarl. It leaps onto the man lying beside her, she draws his sword and spears its coarse fur in the nick of time. The man without a name has fainted, shocked unconscious.

The pregnancy becomes, above all, the two women's concern, but it probably would have been anyway. As it still can be.

It is then that it happens; after having been thin and bony for so long, a sudden dramatic change. His body has begun to swell. His stomach bulges and expands until it is almost as round as hers, his face swells, his feet swell and his fingers grow thick. I write that the child kicks and shifts inside her – however much I have forgotten, I will never forget that feeling – and that she takes his hand and places it on her. His skin has yellowed by now, but she can't see it in the darkness, and maybe she's seeing past the hand itself, seeing her belly through it.

Dramatic writing has often been freeing for me. With prose it was easy to shut myself inside the language and get stuck, but drama had a built-in forward momentum: first this happens, then that and then it's over. I had longed to be swept away by it, but switching between these two forms with this project meant that the forward momentum provided no respite. In fact, it was part of what was holding me back – my awareness of what was to come. When I didn't lose focus because my brain was carrying my thoughts off in another direction or because life was what it was – so unbelievably merciless and dark – I was held back by exactly what could have propelled me forwards. The direction, what was to come. That which lay in waiting.

There was my usual reluctance to leave the text, which was now worse than ever, along with procrastination naturally, avoiding getting to the parts of the story that I didn't want to get to. It frightened me more than the cold, the bears, the wolverines and the husband's fever that kept rising and rising. Again I look at the oblong shape drawn in front of the log cabin in the etching. Instead of continuing with my story (yes, I'm writing 'my story' now), towards what was looming a few steps down the path, I lingered in the source materials and was more frequently visited by the thought that reading them in digital format might not be enough. I got it into my head that I wanted to see and touch the books.

I contacted an administrator at the Bibliothèque National de France who informed me that digitised works weren't available to the general public. One could get special dispensation by proving extraordinary circumstances but I had no desire to. All I wanted was to hold an object that they may have held. Maybe my longing to travel was what made me think about the books as the physical objects I knew them to be, and where they might be found. I constantly thought back to those days in Paris and Roberval, the heat that was so impossible to recall at the end of a long winter, the blazing sun climbing over the tower, how it glistened on the sculptures of the four faces and flared in Aymen's car and on his wristwatch, how it made the cigarette in his hand look so good. That afternoon was etched in me, what had been so diffuse when I was there, the evanescence that arose in spite of the solidity of the building. I had been overwhelmed by the thought of what I was going to do with this and what value it would have when I was finished. It was a premonition of the feeling I'm having as I write; that all I've been doing is destroying, annihilating my own hope about what my words could become.

When it was about time to leave Roberval for the airport in Beauvais, I got it into my head that I should take something away with me. It might have been an attempt to push away the emptiness and the feeling of transience that had entered me. The impulse was familiar and one that I found distasteful, my always wanting something, a thing to hold and own. A souvenir.

It struck me that I could break off a piece of the wall, but I didn't dare. I have a hard time understanding it now, it seems so strange that I had been afraid of an act as simple as picking off a small stone or a crumb of plaster. Who was I afraid of? I stood there a while, vacillating. My daughter came up to me, her phone still in her hand and her eyes glued to it, on her own image I assumed, and asked, without looking at me, if we would be leaving soon. I said I wanted to stay a little longer, that all we'd end up doing was hanging around the airport for longer if we left now, and when she let out a groan, I said that I wanted to see if I could maybe take something with me, if maybe I could take a small piece of the wall.

She looked at me. 'So do it! Why don't you just do it?'

I didn't know what to say. I just stood there. I asked her to take a picture of me instead. I held up two fingers in the air like a V. I was wearing a baseball cap, a marbled grey T-shirt that belonged to her, which I'd borrowed to wear on the trip home, the letters 'NYU' printed in white plastic over the chest – they were what made the shirt so comfortable because you didn't need to wear a bra, the print covered what might otherwise reveal nipples. I probably looked like an American pensioner.

Once she had taken the picture and handed me back the phone, it was as though I could see us from the outside. From above, like on Google Earth. I saw myself and I saw her, and Aymen pacing the far end of the parking lot, and it was as though we were heavenly bodies orbiting each other. Or rather, what I saw was how they were orbiting me, me standing by the tower, paralysed by my own fear of not being able to write about this and ashamed that I was the one guiding this situation, that I had brought her and him to this place because I needed to come. And another thing: how my actions were shaping her future.

'Are we leaving now, or what?' she asked.

She didn't take her eyes off the phone and I think that something about her absent expression and the way her lips were set in that moment bothered me and fuelled the distaste I didn't want to be feeling towards her. She reminded me so much of myself, when I was her age, but also now. My yearning and my hesitation. She sighed loudly and stuffed the phone in her pocket. The battery had died.

'Just do whatever you're going do already!' she exclaimed.

That was it. She didn't swear, wasn't any more unpleasant than this, but her tone was enough to rouse my ire, a trivial rage, the bitterness of which tinged the lovely afternoon, the wall and the succulents and the lush trees, emptying it of all beauty and meaning for me.

I turned my back on her and walked off. It was the wrong move, and yet I took pleasure in it. It was an awful feeling. A fit of temper, the devastating power of which was only trumped by the ensuing shame. 'Come on, then,' I shouted.

'Is it time, madame?' Aymen asked.

'Yes,' I said. 'Let's go.'

She didn't come right away. She was still over by the wall, dragging her feet, she who had nagged at me to leave. I took a deep breath and tried to relax.

It was stuffy in the car, the black leather seat was burning hot. Aymen turned on the AC. Then she arrived. She climbed into the car and sat down, closed the car door, then carefully reached over the console containing still-unopened Evian bottles and placed her fist in my lap.

'Here,' she said.

When she opened her hand I saw a green leaf. It was folded and she must have picked it from the large maple. She sat up straight and fastened her seatbelt. I took the maple leaf and unfolded it. A light grey object was revealed. A small piece of the wall.

I unbuckled my seatbelt so I could hug her. When I'd buckled up again, Aymen turned around in the driver's seat. He reached out his hand to me and smiled. 'I must thank you for this journey now, madame,' he said. 'In case I forget later!'

He let go of my hand, straightened up in the seat and started the engine. The car rolled away from the car park. I looked at the empty road ahead, glittering in the sun, then cast a final glance at the tower and the castle, how it stood there, framed by foliage, in repose and silent, like any other old building.

The man dies in February. The dreariest, most unrelenting month. The year: 1543. Marguerite de Navarre wrote that no one but his wife was with him on the island – because that's how she told her story, she didn't include Damienne – and thanks to her he made his way to heaven:

> At last, however, the husband could no longer endure this nutriment, and by reason of the waters that they drank became so swollen that in a short while he died, and this without any service or consolation save from his wife, she being both his doctor and his confessor; and when he had joyously passed out of the desert into the heavenly country . . .

She must have long known that he was dying, if nothing else Damienne would have known, she had surely seen men die before – but neither of them says anything to him until the very end. I looked at paintings depicting the sacrament of extreme unction to see if the dying usually held their crosses as he did in that one illustration I have of him and her, which I have now found out is from the 1800s, made by the engraver John James Hinchliff. Its relative newness is quite clear, but when I first saw it I didn't reflect much on the style. All I could think about was his appearance, considering the possibility that it was a depiction of him in his last days, that this might have been why he looked the way he did. I read that when one of Marguerite de Navarre's ladies-in-waiting lay dying, she had sat with her until the end so she could witness it, see what death looked like when it occurred. I want to find out more about that moment now and read what she wrote about it afterwards.

As so often happens when it comes to Navarre, I lose myself.

I stray from the subject.

Once he is gone, she closes his eyes and prays for him again. Then she and Damienne set out to dig a hole in the ground near an old tree that had been felled by lightning. I think they choose this place because it's special, using the tree as a marker. They work for days, hacking and digging with his tools and using a few flat stones as spades, as deep as they can go, loosening stones and carrying them away. When the grave is dug, Damienne takes care of the man's clothes. She undresses him garment by garment and sets each one aside until his distorted body is bared; she folds them up and places them among the other things in their storage. After that they carry his body to the grave site. Damienne walks back and fetches the book so they can hold a memorial. She reads. Damienne silently looks upon the man, then starts covering him with earth and stones.

This is when Marguerite de Navarre starts calling her the 'poor woman'. She wrote that she:

> Buried him in the earth as deeply as she was able. Nevertheless the beasts quickly knew of it, and came to eat the dead body; but the poor woman, firing with the arquebuss from her cabin, saved her husband's flesh from finding such a grave.

Thevet mentions that she is filled with grief after the man's death but wrote that she was a person who was 'always making of necessity a virtue' and that she and Damienne defended themselves against the ravening, mad beasts forever attacking them, steadfast with their guns and the dead man's sword, and with the arquebus, which by then she could so skillfully wield that she once shot three bears in a day. And the last bear – this, she told him, was 'as white as an egg'.

I have never been chased by a bear, never felt the breath of a wild animal on my skin, and not even as I was standing in front of the stuffed bears at the hunting museum could I imagine how it must have felt when they caught her scent. How she had to climb trees to escape, make her way down the mountain's crevices, into a narrow ravine, dash straight up a cliff.

I write that this is how she finds herself in the cave.

She doesn't mention any of this to Thevet, or maybe she asks him not to write about it. (She doesn't seem to have mentioned her trophies, either – that she had slit the throats of the bears and all the other animals she had killed and hung their heads in the trees.)

There is no doubt that they would have found the cave because the island is so small, and they must have moved into it because in all likelihood they were used to the mountain caves in southern France: how a grotto could offer cool respite in summer and warmth in winter, much better protection than the log cabin. Elizabeth Boyer refers to the locals she interviewed during her visit to the island, who recounted stories that had been passed down for generations, about how long ago shards of pottery and a bit of a shoe were found deep inside it: exactly the kind of objects that under the right conditions could be preserved for centuries.

I tried to get a sense of how big the cave was, what it smelled like inside the mountain and how sooty it got when they lit a fire; if the fire scorched them and if they could keep it alive without needing to crawl out; if the smoke escaped, as Boyer describes, through a hole in the rock that acted as a natural chimney.

I often googled 'Margaret's cave' but all I seemed to find was information about a cave of the same name in Scotland, named after the Catholic Saint Margaret. Then one day, right as I was about to give up, I caught sight of a photo of a young girl and an older woman on a rocky beach. I clicked on the image and came to a blog post about the young girl's visit to the island where her grandmother lived. Among other things they were going to visit the cave, she wrote, and I started reading faster, as though I knew it contained something that I was looking for even if it was unclear what. I skimmed the description of their outing, until I came to the last paragraph and stopped. It said that the cave had collapsed and was no longer accessible.

Only when I read that did I realise how much I had wanted to go there and crawl in and lie down, deep inside against the mountain.

Thevet wrote that the man died when she was close to full term. It was one of the short, simple sentences that with all its brutality bound me to *La Cosmographie Universelle*. These few words in the midst of everything else left me with all my questions about how it happened and what she was thinking. In them lay the entire drama, as I saw it, and not in what he chose to focus on: page after page of exposition on spirits and phantoms and how she ceaselessly prayed to God to make them disappear.

It was the same way with the birth. To me it was among the most central parts of the story, but none of the sources delved into it. At most the references to the birth are glancing; a pregnancy progresses and a child is born and that's all there is to it. Thevet mentions it in passing. On first reading, it was shocking, a mockery, but now I think: of course, they were used to women giving birth to children and that being that, and without much knowledge of how a birth transpired. And she wasn't alone then either, so maybe they didn't think it was significant. Or was it because André Thevet and François de Belleforest were men? Marguerite de Navarre omits the birth in that she doesn't mention the child, it isn't part of her story.

It was in March, the same time of year as it was for us. On the island, winter was far from over, but here it had grown milder during the days when we were hanging around, waiting for the child that was to be born. I had packed away my long underwear in a bag that I was supposed to take up to the attic along with the old down jacket that I still wore in wintertime, even though I hated it. Most mornings after I'd dropped the children at school I sat with my computer at a café with an upstairs that was quiet because many other people went there to work, and from the tables by the window, you could see out over the water coursing through our city, the bridges perpetually under construction, and the heavy lidded sky.

Whatever I did I kept my phone near to me and the ringer on so I would be sure to hear it. In the nights, I was a light sleeper. I woke up again and again, checking the phone. I wanted to be prepared.

Still, I wasn't the least bit worried, because I remembered how it had been when my oldest daughter was born over fifteen years ago. Thinking about my own first birth calmed me, not because it had been easy, but because it had been very difficult. I had labour pains for two days but couldn't have any anaesthesia and wasn't allowed to move around as I pleased because I had a fever, and a number of machines

connected to me. All I could do was lie in the bed and take
the pain. It was like being run over repeatedly until I was in
pieces: my body lurched and careened from side to side; I
wailed and screamed until I lost my voice; my vocal cords
burned and stung and emitted no sound.

It must have looked awful from the outside, but inside
was a clear stability. I wasn't afraid, and the knowledge of
it, of how labour could look nothing like it felt, calmed me
when I thought of my sister-in-law's birth. I only worried
that I might be plagued by the longing for another child
when I saw her in labour, that my sense of myself as a
person who had her biological urges under control was an
illusion. I was probably as driven by them as anyone else,
only that it was difficult for me to see their effects under-
neath all the other layers.

I asked myself what it was that made people like me, who
already had several children, want more. Was it a wish to
again be close to a pre-verbal being who was not yet marked
by civilisation's and one's own faults and shortcomings, and
to get it right this time? I didn't consider that I couldn't have
become pregnant even if I'd wanted to because I hadn't had
my period for months. It had cast a dismal shadow over me,
but I'd managed to suppress it, or to suppress what it implied.

When the day came and we were in the delivery room with
all the machines and resources and the midwife was going
through the various phases of birth, I understood that the

longing I felt wasn't about having another child and watching it grow up. It might sound strange, but what I longed
for was the birth itself. Like a wildfire, its wake had left the
core of me scorched, and I suspected I wanted to encounter
this anew. Birth is fundamental but also unlike anything else
in life; a door through which all of existence passes and yet
a total anomaly, to no longer exist as anything but a hole
through which the new emerges, an opening for the life that
is meant to continue after mine has ended. I dissolved when I
gave birth to my daughter – my physical body collapsed and
my mind seemed to have been pulled so deep into its schism
that in the end I was more dead than alive. I found myself on
the side of existence that belongs to the dead and the other,
the place where what is to begin living waits, and when I
think about it now I can't understand how I could imagine
life continuing as before.

Afterwards, something mysterious had happened. On an
intellectual level, I was aware of the pain I had been in, but
I had no physical memory of it. And this remains true. I can
sense how the first real contractions tore at my flesh from
the inside, but when I tried to recall how it then intensified and gained even more strength, I can't remember any
actual pain, only unspeakably positive sensations, like pure
pleasure. A doctor I met after the fact explained that this was
because of a misfiring in the brain that could occur after a
complicated birth, where the memory of it is connected to

the centre for pleasure instead of the centre for pain, so it becomes associated with gratification. It is a survival mechanism so that people who had a near-death experience during the birth of a child could find it in themselves to live on and perhaps even continue to reproduce. Unless the memory was suppressed, this would be impossible.

I usually tell this story when I end up in conversations about birth and I always think that I'm repeating myself, that I get into the memory and the pain and the pleasure in a way that makes me feel silly, and yet I can't resist. I've had to talk about my daughter's birth in order to make it real, like you can't help but recount the dream you had last night, even though you know most people think it's boring to hear about other people's dreams because they're not real. What I'd experienced wasn't really real, either. Like a dream, it had arisen within me.

I imagined that Damienne had brought many children into the world, that she knew all about it. She was with her through it all, in the cave. Together they managed, just as we would. She gave birth in March or possibly in early April 1543, according to what she told Thevet. He wrote:

After she bore the child, and baptised it in her fashion, in the name of God, without ceremonies, we see that fortune gave her another blow.

It's an early November morning. Six months have passed. She wakes to cries, sharp nails digging into her skin. She turns to face him and gets in the right position, cupping her hand around his head when he latches, feeling his hair against her palm, the hair that has gone as rough as straw and falls off his head when she touches it. Does she know what this means? Damienne must have known and I wonder if this knowledge was too much for her. Or did she think that by doing what she did she'd be able to change the outcome?

He's crying again. His tongue smacks against his dry palate and when she opens her eyes to see if he's getting any milk, she notices that the space behind him is empty. The old woman isn't in her spot. She says her name aloud in the dark, but there's no reply. She looks around, but she's nowhere to be seen. He complains, still hungry. Forever hungry it seems, even though she has been feeding him morsels of dried bear meat which she has chewed and softened in her mouth.

She straps him to her back and takes the sword and crawls out onto the cliff's ledge. Morning has yet to break but the island is waking up and, in the now-waning night, the first snow has fallen. She feels the snow under her fingers as she climbs down the mountain, slowly so as not to slip and fall with him. It looks like fog at first, blanketing the rocks and ground, thin and barren in places, thicker on the tree branches and in the glade. It grows lighter as she walks. She's looking in every direction and shouting; her shouts echo in the ravine and mingle with his shrill cries.

First she catches sight of the clothes. They're in a crevice at the foot of the mountain. She picks them up and beats the snow off them and when she stops on her way up the path in order to fold them and wedge them under her arm, she sees. At that distance and at first glance it's but an incongruous shape and colour. She takes a seat on a stone, doesn't look in its direction but still she sees: like a pale, snow-dusted slab that hadn't been there before. She sits as long as she dares before she has to take care of it. The animals are encroaching. (Thevet wrote that they could smell their way to her from anywhere. He wrote: *She was a real plum for them.*)

Her son wakes up in his bundle and she rises from the stone and cautiously tries to rock him to sleep again. Briefly he falls silent but then his whimpers become an insistent whine, the kind that can lure animals, and she has to unswaddle him and offer him her breast. She wishes he could take hold of it himself, so that she could keep her free hand on the sword now that she doesn't have a firearm with her, but he needs help. He latches and she looks down at him, his bent arm and moving fingers, spreading in pace with the pressure of his tongue against her nipple. The noises he makes calm her, him eating.

When he's done, she hears a rustle in the thicket. The sword is in her hand, but she doesn't have the energy to strap him to her back again. Instead she holds him upright, his head under her chin, his tiny body held like a shield. She listens, but hears nothing more.

After a rest, she straps him to her back again. Only once she's done with that does she turn her gaze to the white-ness in the thicket, slowly, to get used to the sight. Even from this distance she can see that her back broke when it hit the ground. She gets up and starts walking, and when she gets closer she sees the marks on the naked body where it slammed against the mountain on its way down.

Does it even cross her mind that she could leave it there, that this isn't Damienne, but her flesh, that she could leave it to the animals and let them take care of it? What difference would it have made? It would have been so much easier. *Why can't you just do that instead*, I wondered, but presumably it had to do with something beyond my comprehension, about God and about the hope of being forgiven.

I write that she bends down carefully and grabs hold of one wrist and starts dragging the body, the sword in her other hand. The body leaves a blush-red trail through the white, the snow mixed with blood. It seems familiar to me – perhaps the wild strawberries the children pluck in the afternoons, the only berries that grow here now, how they look as leftovers, mashed in a pool of cream.

In *La Cosmographie Universelle,* death is a path that leads away from the world. Thevet wrote that her servant followed in the footsteps of her husband during the sixteenth or seventeenth month on the island, but this is all he says. He doesn't write about how it happened. For a long time I assumed this was because Damienne's death was uninteresting to them in the way that her life had been, but there's another reason not to mention it. Marguerite presumably didn't tell him how she died.

Surely it would have been a relief for her to talk about this, along with everything else? There was probably a lot said during that interview that was off the record, but when it came to this perhaps she had to hold her tongue, perhaps she wouldn't dare ask a former Franciscan monk to forgive the worst of the cardinal sins. She had to keep quiet so as not to dishonour Damienne's memory.

According to Elizabeth Boyer, the islanders she met had passed down a story through the generations, a story about how one of the marooned from the French expedition fell from the highest cliff on the mountain, where there is a sharp vertical drop. She wrote in *A Colony of One* that it lies just east of the cave. It is high and sheer and it would be easy for a person frail with age to fall if she were on her way up the side that lent itself to climbing, especially if that person were dressed in long skirts and 'caught in a gust of wind':

> But perhaps Damienne, too, may have reached the end of her endurance. Perhaps like many who are old and poor today, she dreaded the onset of winter with its unendurable cold.

I had read that there was a lack of funding for research into the theory that children bear greater resemblance to their fathers in the beginning, but I seemed to see evidence of it everywhere: infants who had inherited their fathers most striking features even when they weren't the type you expected to see in a newborn's face. It was said to be nature's way of preventing the menfolk from killing their offspring. (Or was it to get them to care for them?)

When she held the child out in front of her she would see the man without a name in him, like I thought I could see a man whose name I didn't know either when I held my sister-in-law's son in my arms, as she lay in the bed, saying that this was the beginning of a new life that would be filled with worry. I stood by the window and felt his breath against my skin, gentle yet heavy.

I didn't know how long we'd been at the hospital – the days flowed together for me – but when I looked out over the car park I saw that spring had arrived. The ground was dry and the sun was high. Its shine was more intense and flashed on the asphalt and shimmered in the thornbushes.

That same morning I had lain with my phone on the vinyl-covered sofa in the delivery room and seen a Facebook post linking to an article about the changing of seasons in this part of the world. It said that for winter to be considered to have passed, a rise in temperature between zero and ten degrees over a period of seven days and seven nights is required and even if it drops again, spring is said to have sprung on that first day. I wanted to concentrate on the feeling of finally being able to hold the child, his tiny vertebrae at the round of his back under my hand, the thin skin of his chest rising and falling with his breath. But my thoughts were in the way. I was thinking about arriving back at home and seeing my own children and taking out their spring wardrobe and the air being clement and clear as I walked them to school the next day, and that it would feel as self-evident as the gentle weight of his vital body in my arms; like something I couldn't believe I had ever doubted.

With spring's arrival, it became easier to write. In spite of all the thoughts I'd had, this change made me feel ridiculous. Was that it? Was it really this simple? Our home was cast in a different light. The apartment seemed worn and claustrophobic and the dirt in every room was revealed. Dust rose from the piles of books stacked all over the place and whirled in the sun when it shone in. On the skirting boards were dark spots where the white paint had been rubbed off and the wood was peeking through.

When I read what I'd written, it seemed to be obscured by the darkness that once was, as shut in and petrified as I had felt. The children spoke of summer and all that we would do and I realised that the thought of it was not enough. It used to help, but it was different now. Now, everything was happening so fast. I knew the warm season would pass in a flash, barely registering, and when it was over, the cold and dark would return with undiminished strength.

I write that she digs the second grave next to the first. It must have been the only way. He is still on her back. He has stopped crying and is resting, looking out, head to the side, roughly rocked by her movements. At first I thought she'd be able to work without needing to watch him: I imagined her taking the sling she had made from the clothes of the dead and hanging it from a branch, out of the animals' reach. I hadn't yet thought of the birds of prey and perhaps at this stage neither had she, but over the course of sixteen or seventeen months they must have appeared to her often, making her fully aware of their presence and how easy it would be for them to snatch him away if he were hanging in a tree.

The other option is leaving him at the back of the cave and sealing off the opening, perhaps with a large rock. She may have done this, especially during nap time. Later, when she was watching over the newly dug grave, she'd be able to hear him wake up and start screaming, and before he'd learned to roll over and crawl, he was probably safe in the cave. Or was he? Were there animals that could find their way in if they caught his scent?

I write that she covers the old woman's naked body with as much earth and clay as she can dig up and fills the hole. Then she has to try to clear the trail of blood as well, but as she works, she realises that it's probably too late, the animals are already drawing near. She sits on the ledge outside the cave in the remains of the day, at the ready with the long rifle in her hands and the gunpowder beside her. Below her is the island and the forest, black and white and beautiful. She looks down into the trees and shoots as soon as she sees an animal nearing the graves.

Three wolverines arrive, one right after the next. She hits one of them and the other two turn and scurry back in among the trees. The explosions and her son's shrieks inside the cave echo across the island and the smoke from the fire mixes with the gun smoke whirling around her and the mountain's haze. The wolverine writhes and twitches like a fish, a large hole in its thick fur at the jaw, white teeth shining in the ravaged flesh. As its movements cease, the blood seeps across the white ground, colouring it again.

She lowers her arquebus and lies down with it on the dank rock. The screams from inside the cave have waned, the boy is only crying now and, between his sniffles and gulps, it's silent. All is silent, nothing moves, not even a tree as the wind is still too. She lies there, recharging, mustering the energy to crawl in and comfort him. She knows how much it will hurt. Even though she has been able to eat her fill of late, the milk in her breasts is ebbing away.

According to Thevet, what is about to happen happens 'a little time afterward'. I calculated that they barely had a month together after Damienne's passing. I thought it must have been hard, but that the time would have flown by because she was alone with him and didn't have anyone to help lighten her load. She would have to do everything herself: protect and carry, look out and listen for animals, keep watch, lull and try to feed him.

He is six, maybe seven months old. He can grab hold of what's in reach, he can roll from his stomach to his back and crawl a short distance. He can smile and laugh. She reads to him from the little book, the New Testament with the ragged spine, the gold plates blackened, and she sings a song she remembers hearing as a child.

In the evenings she's beyond tired – from all she has to do each day and the thought of tomorrow, even more of the same. She listens to him babble and to his breathing, caresses his stomach to ease the swelling.

No one mentions this, but by now his stomach must be swollen. I write that she knows what's going to happen, but I think there's something inside her resisting it, refusing it.

An unusually early hot summer was forecast. When the city became unbearable, I brought the youngest ones out here. At the end of the bus line were open fields, the sky above them blue, horses were grazing in a pasture and in the ditch running along it was the wreck of an old rusty tractor. We got off there and started walking in the sunshine. I took off my jacket and took theirs too. They were carrying their own backpacks and only when we arrived at the side road that leads to our summer house did it occur to me that this was the first time they had walked here from the bus. They were lagging slightly behind me, and I heard them talking about the forest on either side of us, about which part was the most beautiful and most like a fairy tale. The north side was dark, the ground wet and marshy around the roots of the aspens and firs, but on the south side the trees were fewer with bushy moss between them, bathed in rays of light.

I could hardly believe that they were already big enough to walk the whole way, and I hadn't even given it a second thought; I had taken it for granted. At the roadside grew nettles and meadowsweet, a pair of brimstones fluttered past us and as we neared our plot of land we spotted the old overgrown apple tree, its gnarled grey branches reaching in every direction. On the meadow, between the trees and the road, red clovers were starting to blossom and up on the hill, behind the house, the tall pines stretched skyward. Protection, I thought.

The children ran the last stretch and I let them fetch the house key from the hiding place and unlock the door and carry our things in while I turned on the water and dragged out the garden furniture and the old grill. Next to the wall the sunflowers we had sown had come up and the glassed-in veranda was hot from the sun that had been blazing through the windows. I put the food in the refrigerator, swept and aired the place and unpacked my things; I put the books I'd brought with me on the veranda table and placed my computer next to them, and pulled out the chair that had been there, waiting for me.

I'd never felt entirely comfortable being alone with the children for longer spells and especially not here, where the loneliness seemed more palpable than in the city, but once we had got everything in order and they'd settled in with their iPads and books and rediscovered everything they'd left behind the summer before, I noticed a change. I wasn't worried, nor was I afraid of work taking over and me ending up at the computer and avoiding listening to them or helping them because I didn't want to do anything but write, because nothing that happened between us or inside me mattered as long as the text existed.

I fried up fish fingers for the children and after they'd eaten, I did the dishes and cleared up the kitchen. Later, as I was reading and writing, tossing an occasional glance at the road and across our property, everything seemed new and different, but not dreadfully so. On the contrary, it was pleasant. As usual, the mock orange plant had shot up like a high, thick wall along the veranda, with a criss-cross of branches and new shoots inside the greenery. Its scent reached everywhere. By the gutter under the roof a pair of swallows were flitting in and out of the nest they built there each year. The rapping of a lone woodpecker high up in a tree echoed through the countryside. It sounded like a tree branch creaking.

I went out onto the balcony to try and catch sight of it and, as I was looking around me, how she had managed to survive on the island no longer seemed incomprehensible. What surrounded her was still threatening, but it was alive, in the same way as what was alive around me would continue living regardless of me, regardless of all of us who were in the cottage and whatever our futures held. Even when everything changed, something would remain. Perhaps the woodpecker and the pines, perhaps just the clay in the earth and the hills behind us, the light that came and went in the sky, something of all of this would remain.

I went back inside and clicked my way to the end of Thevet's book and its index, which I hadn't looked at in a while, his table of 'remarkable things' around the world and on which pages they could be found: a buffalo described as a monster, a haltered giraffe being led by indigenous people, a group of 'savage' women who have cut off a man's leg and strung him up in a tree, a sable-tooth shark with fur, a volcano in the jungle and a school of wide-winged fish flying over the water. The midnight sun, the northern lights, a breadfruit tree.

Suddenly it was clear to me that what Thevet wanted to depict was the world – not a lone woman in it. It's what I'd been thinking all along, but in that moment the meaning of it changed. André Thevet had been recording what went on regardless of her or anyone else.

In that moment the world around her was also cast in a new light. Until then it had seemed so abstract. Or rather, I hadn't seen it. It was as though I'd been blind to it, as though she and her personage had drawn me in so close that I hadn't been able to see anything but the constant threat of every danger. Now I saw it at once, what had allowed her to survive. I heard the birds and the trees, saw the forest and the islets and the empty sea with its open horizon, I saw the nuances in the granite and I could feel the freshness of the air. I knew I could no longer avoid what I hadn't wanted to reach.

I think it's a day like any other. She has crawled onto the cliff's ledge with him in her arms, feeling the gentle pulse of his breath, the breath she has spent so much time listening to, against her chest. And then it's not there anymore. I don't know if it's sudden, but it ends. It falls still. The breathing ceases and all falls still, all that has been.

I knew that the death of a child was different then, more normal and understandable and perhaps not as remarkable as I perceived it to be – because it was more common, and so one might prepare for this eventuality, but also because they had one eye trained on eternity, a concept to which I, along with most people I knew, had no connection. Still I couldn't accept how Thevet approached it. He handled the death as he had the birth: so quickly resolved, in passing, in the midst of everything else he had to note and report – which is per- haps to say everything he considered to be his true subject.

I pulled up Thevet's story to re-read it, that lone sentence that I had read so many times before. I searched around it for something more, but there was nothing. It was so harsh, so raw. It was as though to him life and death were equals, delivery and departure but passages leading in this or that direction. What for me underpinned the whole story and inflamed it with white-hot horror, he'd interjected as a subordinate clause. He wrote only that it was during the sixteenth or seventeenth month on the island that Damienne passed and shortly thereafter the child followed the same path as the two who had gone before.

As long as his body is warm it's as though the stillness hadn't yet arrived. She keeps holding him. She must have long known what was coming, perhaps was waiting for it to happen. Damienne must have known, and perhaps this is what she had wanted to avoid – 'avoid' as in not have to see it happen because she couldn't take any more, or 'avoid' as in remove herself. I don't know. But it's reasonable to assume that she knew; that it lay ahead of her as it had lain ahead of me. Or is this idea my way of trying to create balance, considering everything I read about how women in the past weren't attached to their children like we are?

I wonder how long she sat with him and what she did after, and how. The thought made me feel ill. It pained me. It was what it was: I often felt physically unwell when writing about certain things. I needed to go out and get some air. The children were old enough now that they could be left alone for a while and also to say if they didn't want to be. Their iPad time was over, they had built a blanket fort in the room and they were inside it playing cards. I walked into the room, turned on the TV and said that I was going for a walk.

'You can watch TV while I'm gone, if you like.'

My son dashed out of the fort so quickly it collapsed. 'And can we have apples?' he asked.

'Yeah, apples!' his sister exclaimed.

They had been asking for apples all afternoon but hadn't been given any because I didn't want them to fill up before dinner, and they weren't going to get any now either. 'Not now,' I said. 'You can have one when I come back, OK?'

They grumbled and faced the television. I left through the front door, but as I was standing on the doorstep I had a thought, went back through the hall and into the kitchen and took the basket of apples from the old wooden stove we didn't use anymore and put it on top of a high cabinet – even I had to stand on a stool – well out of the children's reach. When they were smaller the cabinet had been cluttered with things that we needed to hand but didn't want them to reach, sharp things like paring knives and carving knives and can openers, and now I didn't want them to be able to access the apples. They often ate so quickly, barely chewing, and it frightened me to think of what could happen if they ate apples alone in the cottage.

It was still hot outside. I walked down to the road and did the short loop, which begins with a view of the water and the bay, a small coastal inlet, and then I veered off on the path down by the dock where the reeds were dense and high, their downy plumes unmoving. I crossed the meadow where the Midsummer pole would soon stand and walked through a copse and arrived at the lesser path that leads to the headland. I was thinking that it wasn't possible to know if it felt less horrific to her because it was more common then, an experience many had shared.

And of course she was all alone.

It was after her son had disappeared down the path the others had trodden before him that things became difficult. She had told André Thevet during their interview that this period, when no one else was with her, was the worst. It was then the visions came. Over the next two months, December and January or January and February, she was embattled with monsters, he wrote. They haunted her as strange hallucinations in the light of night; demons found their way into the cave and would not cease wreaking havoc until she prayed to God. She lay there, repeating her prayers in the hope that they'd disappear.

Everywhere it is written that this is how she persevered. To Marguerite de Navarre, who set the new faith's simplicity against Catholicism's and the Church's many compulsory rituals, it seemed so free and pure; Navarre seems almost envious when she writes that the woman lived a life which was on the outside no better than an animal's, but on the inside was that of an angel, insofar as 'she passed her time in reading, meditations, prayers and orisons, having a glad and happy mind in a wasted and half-dead body'.

I spot 'half-dead' throughout my notes now. The words pop up everywhere.

Did she think death would come as a relief? Did she lie inside the cave waiting for it, like an animal waiting to die? At some point she must have gone outside, and I wondered if what she saw out there was part of what was keeping her alive; everything on the island that was so remarkable to me and surely was to her, as well. I walked to the bathing rocks where the sun had heated up the rough slabs. The water closest to them was transparent, but bluer in the far distance, and a red-flowering grass I'd never seen before was growing in the crevices down by the water's edge.

I stood a while on the rock furthest out and watched the water move between the islands and out by the narrows. Then there the pain was again. I suddenly felt dizzy and when I sat on the bedrock I saw that my legs were streaked with blood. I took off my underwear, blood-soaked, and my shoes, only slightly spattered, and walked into the water and let it wash the red away. At first I held up my dress, but then I pulled it off and laid it on a large rock within easy reach if anyone were to come by. I took a step out into the cool water. It reached my waist. I walked further out and felt the pebbles and seaweed against my calves and my feet sinking deeper into the soft sandy ground. I leaned forwards and let go, swam a stroke, and let myself sink beneath the surface.

When she's standing on the beach, at the water's edge, the year is 1544, the month November. Does she know this? She has crawled out of the cave, made her way down the mountain, to the shore. Something compelled her.

In the drawing in *La Cosmographie Universelle*, a large ship and two smaller sailboats lay in the water beyond the island, but in reality there were mostly never boats in the area. Thevet himself wrote that not a single ship passed by in the first eight months, but perhaps the illustrator hadn't wanted to consider chronology and decided to allow everything to exist all at once. But in that case they've left someone out. However I look at it, I only count three people on the page.

From June until September crews from southern Europe fished for cod in the waters around the island and sometimes they were late; at least, they were on this occasion, and it's not impossible that it had happened before, that others had seen her standing on the rocks on the beach, but had decided not to come near. In my visions she was as pale as I was, but judging by what I had read, her skin had a dark tan and was grimy from earth and soot, and the sailors who saw her are said to have explained that they didn't dare approach the island because they thought it was a troll or a devil standing there, waving its arms at them.

In Tale LXVII it's a boat from Roberval's fleet that is sailing by:

> . . . *when one of the ships of the armament was passing by the island, those that were looking that way perceived some smoke, which reminded them of the persons who had been left there, and they resolved to go and see what God had done with them.*

Marguerite de Navarre wrote that the poor woman had seen the ship draw nigh and dragged herself to the shore and there they found her when they moored. Was it to further appease Jean-François de la Rocque de Roberval that she had put it this way? Throughout her life she had been taught to keep men in good spirits: perhaps she thought she could manipulate his reaction by turning him into her saviour, so that her fate lay entirely in his hands – and he wouldn't be portrayed as unreasonable. I wondered if she saw this as a way of giving Marguerite a chance to stay alive after what had happened. And was this also why she claimed Roberval was her source? Who knows what was fabricated and what was written bearing the reality of the situation in mind, or if the story was part of an attempt to recast reality. It's obvious, really, and I realise that the same can be said of what I have written:

> *After giving praise to God, she brought them to her poor cottage and showed them on what she had lived during her abode in that place. This would have seemed to them impossible of belief, but for their knowledge that God is as powerful to feed His servants in a desert as at the greatest banquet in the world.*

Actually, it was a fishing boat from Normandy. It had got stuck in the estuary and stayed behind, blown in by an unexpected storm. The crew was in a hurry to depart before the winter, but when they caught sight of her signalling on the beach, they headed for the island.

I imagine that they're consulting *Le Routier de Jean Alfonse,* which had recently been printed following Jean Alfonse de Saintonge and the expedition's return to Paris, in a first edition in which he has given the group of islands yet another name. He calls them *Les îles de la Demoiselle,* 'the young noblewoman's islands'.

When I've thought about who was actually on her side, if anyone was, I often compared the cartographers André Thevet and Jean Alfonse, chiefly because of how they named the island. Unlike Thevet, Alfonse was already famous in his lifetime. His status likely made it easier for him to speak

frankly with Roberval, questioning his decisions and perhaps even discussing them with the king. I would like to
think that it is Jean Alfonse who saves her with that name,
but perhaps the Norman fishermen weren't in possession
of his *routier*; perhaps they were simply unafraid, the sight
of her didn't frightened them, so they steered the boat to
the island and went ashore.

They explain to her that they must leave at once so as not
to get caught in the winter weather. She begs them to wait
so she can raise a cross over the graves, but once that is done
she has second thoughts.

I might suggest that she had truly grown fond of the island,
though not in the way I imagined, but rather because it had
become her home, a home for her family. André Thevet
wrote that she is overwhelmed by a desire to stay among
her own and die there, and I wonder what is said in the brief
time the sailors spend waiting for her that changes her mind.
Something must have persuaded her to board their vessel, a
little open fishing boat full of cod, and accompany them all
the way across the ocean.

It was easy for her to then disappear. Women weren't entered into the national registry in France – a girl's life wasn't noted and, just as easily as she could be annihilated by someone else, she could vanish of her own free will.

She ceases to be as soon as she arrives back in France. Perhaps this is what she wanted for herself or someone may have advised her accordingly, perhaps Marguerite de Navarre. Tale LXVII ends when the fishing boat reaches La Rochelle:

> *And when they had made known to the inhabitants the faithfulness and endurance of this woman, she was very honourably received by all the ladies, who gladly sent their daughters to her to learn to read and write. In this honest calling she maintained herself for the rest of her life, having no other desire save to admonish every one to love and trust Our Lord, and setting forth as an example the great compassion that He had shown towards her.*

After this the bards re-enter the picture. The narrators. Simontault says to the women that, having heard him tell this story, they can't possibly suggest he doesn't wish to exalt women's virtues. In a way, this was a happy ending, but I hated how everything she did was ascribed to God's mercy. Giving God all the credit. I remember how angry it made me when I realised that it probably wasn't Marguerite de Navarre's invention alone, but was perhaps her own reasoning as well, in spite of all that had come to pass.

I no longer think of it this way. What made God seem, well, what can I say, more *plausible* to me isn't hard to see. It is the passage of time, time leaving me behind at an ever-increasing speed, but also surrendering something in return.

It seemed a touch thoughtless of Marguerite de Navarre to suggest that she knew what had happened to Roberval's young cousin if there might be a risk that he was in pursuit of her in some way. So does this mean that what she wrote was a fabrication? I felt confused and a little disappointed because her being able to devote the rest of her life to teaching other young women to read and write may have been a form of revenge for her. But then I remembered how much time had passed between Navarre writing and the publication of *The Heptameron*. It was one of the comforts in all of this and yet it had slipped my mind. When the stories were finally published, Marguerite de Navarre was long dead and Roberval an old man whose time had passed. And perhaps the ending wasn't as she had written it; perhaps it was wishful thinking, but I like to think that she – the queen, the author – had taken care of the sinner.

She may have been the one who wanted to no longer exist. It could have been clear to her early on that she would never be able to show her face at court again, perhaps not even return to France. Perhaps it was something the fishermen said to her during their crossing, perhaps she came to the conclusion herself, perhaps it was something of which Marguerite de Navarre had to convince her. Navarre believed in honour, not in revenge, this much is clear from all that she has written and that has been written about her, but I was more inclined to think she would want revenge – and realising that revenge would not be hers must have come as a grave disappointment.

It disappointed everyone who heard this tale. We wanted revenge.

But no requisitions were ever made for the regions and possessions that had belonged to her to be returned by Jean-François de la Rocque de Roberval, and no legal action was ever taken against him. Considering what she had done and the laws of the time, this constituted a protection for her, to again be swallowed by the void and vanish without a trace. It was a question of her continued survival and how the rest of her life would be.

But if she'd had a choice, would she have wanted to disappear?

It seems so strange now that someone would want to choose silence and not have their story told, rather than welcome the spotlight. Yet she had told André Thevet. How she had chosen him, or how he had sought her out, was a peculiar point in all this. If she wanted to keep a low profile, or was being hidden by Navarre, how had he contacted her and what had he told Roberval about it? Had she met him before, maybe during the preparations at the castle in Roberval, or didn't she know that he and Roberval were friends? Might they not have been friends? Did André Thevet keep his interview with her secret for the thirty years it took him to finish *La Cosmographie Universelle*? Did he change anything in it after Roberval's death, when he knew that the man could no longer punish him or her?

The bedrock was still hot when I left the water, but the sun had disappeared behind the trees across the bay and twilight had fallen. I dressed quickly and headed home, cutting through the forest by the meadow and taking the shortest path up to the road. There was a rustle in the thicket; a large moose strolled right past me. I looked up and saw several of them on the hills all around; they were walking around nibbling on branches hanging from the trees. I had never seen so many so close to the road before.

With my every step it darkened. When I reached the crown of the hill at the turn leading to the cottage, I sped up. I hurried down the gravel path and when I was at the house I ran up the steps to the glass veranda and walked in and saw my son standing in the middle of the room. He had gotten up, presumably because he'd heard my footsteps on the gravel or on the terrace, and now was standing next to the collapsed fort.

As I came in, he sat down and looked at me. 'Why didn't you come?' he exclaimed. 'It's almost dark!'

For a split second I thought he looked despairing. I hugged him, sat down and pulled him into my lap and held him. He

was so light, so delicate and slim. His sister took her eyes off
the TV and looked at us. I was about to ask them to turn it off
and go and brush their teeth so we could go to bed and read,
but then I remembered the apples I promised them. I got up,
went to the kitchen and took down the basket, selected two
apples, which I washed and dried and gave to them. Then I
lit a fire in the fireplace and, after I had put them to bed and
they had fallen asleep, I went out on the veranda again.

It was dark. Everything had hushed and found peace. In
here nothing could be heard but the crackling fire. Its light
flickered across the room and reflected in the veranda windows and the glass doors, making it look like small fires
were burning all around me. I opened *The Heptameron* and
as I flipped through it, I remembered that Marguerite de
Navarre had also lost a child, or three rather, because she
had also given birth to twins who died just a few hours after
delivery. I hadn't found anything about the twins, but one
of the loose pages I picked up from the pile on the table said
that *The Mirror of the Sinful Soul*, the book that came to pose
a threat to her safety because it led to her being accused of
heresy, was written out of sorrow – after the son she had
given birth to in July 1530 had died, five months later. When
I saw his name it startled me: Jean. It's what I'd been calling
the son she'd birthed on the island.

Thevet doesn't mention the child's gender in his books,
which could mean that it was a girl, a meaningless child, but

it's more likely that his silence supports the thesis that she gave birth to a boy. It would have been risky to make this fact known: to birth a son was to be blessed by an heir – and her son wasn't just anybody. She was the first person who managed to establish a lasting European settlement in North America and he was the first white man to be born there; the first of the French sons of which the mission had spoken. If the relatives of the man without a name found out, if they had learned of his birth, his death would have upset them. Maybe they would address it with the king and take action, demand compensation for their loss or even an investigation into how Roberval had managed the expedition. François de Belleforest does write that the child she gave birth to was a son. Maybe he didn't consider it to be a risk because he fictionalised, and kept so much else secret. Maybe he didn't care. He probably didn't think his story would be read side-by-side with the others, and that in doing so it could be deduced what was 'true' and what was not.

Marguerite de Navarre had at least one personal experience of how it doesn't pay to speak about the violence of men. The primary purpose of her stories wasn't to honour Boccaccio or help her brother recover from illness, but to break the rules of storytelling by depicting violence from the vulnerable woman's point of view. The motif of attack recurs again and again in her writing, again and again and in different forms she wrote about what the admiral did to her. I wished I had understood it sooner, that I had known it was this experience, and the experience of men as animals – that they were pigs? – that sparked her writing. *The Heptameron* was a result of this. It was why she wrote, I thought. For women's flesh and blood.

Fiction and anonymity, the common name, made it possible for her to protect and hide her young namesake while telling her story. But perhaps she did leave something like a clue behind. On one occasion in late 1544, right around when Marguerite returns to France, Navarre's treasurer is said to have placed an order on behalf of the court in Pau for a complete wardrobe for one *demoiselle de la Roche* who had recently arrived at court and who the queen had decided to take in. 'If she had a hundred daughters I would take them all,' is what Navarre is said to have said about the woman and her sudden appearance. Something quaked in me when I read that and for a second I was thrown back into the question of her identity, before I remembered that it no longer mattered who she was.

She could have been so many people.

Another possible connection between them was that of writer and reader. In *The Heptameron* the conclusion delivered by one of the bards is how women should relinquish the company of men and instead devote themselves entirely to caring for their own souls. I wondered if she had read the book, if Marguerite de Navarre had allowed her to see her story and, if so, what did she think? It's likely that she was still alive when the book came out. Roberval was. Barely a year of his life remained. He was referred to by name in the story, but this didn't mean he'd read it. He can't have read André Thevet's or François de Belleforest's stories of his exploits, because they were only published after he had been dead for fifteen years. She could have been in her fifties or somewhere around there, if she was still alive. This I will never know.

As I saw it, all of this writing was a form of retaliation, if not revenge. Even if Marguerite de Navarre had wanted Marguerite de la Rocque to keep silent about what had happened, she was speaking for her through Tale LXVII,

as she had spoken for so many other women in the vast
book that she had authored – and François de Belleforest
and André Thevet did the same, I thought, whatever their
own take on it was.

I had one last order of business before we left Paris for Roberval and caught our flight home. It was already scorching in the morning of that day. The small room we'd occupied over the weekend was on the top floor, with only the attic above us; when I woke up, I pushed the high slim window wide open and was struck by the heat and the fuggy smell of croissants baking in a café, rising from the street. I could see into the apartments across the way, and above them the black tin roofs, the sky. Screams and laughter rang out. My daughter had woken up and was sitting in bed with her phone, the source of the sound: kids partying, their hoarse, clangy voices trying to drown each other out. I picked my headphones up off the floor and handed them to her.

While I waited for her to get ready I packed our things, then I took out my phone and opened Google Maps; the square I was going to was only a short walk from the hotel. Place Joachim du Bellay, as it was called now, named after a Renaissance poet who had devoted his life to trying to resurrect the classical art of poetry, but when Roberval was there it had gone by the name of Place des Innocents. It was where the Cimetière des Innocents had lain, the cemetery that had been the city's oldest and largest up until 1786, when it was closed, the corpses exhumed and moved to catacombs. I had shown my daughter a photo of them, rows of skulls and skeletons still on public display in underground tunnels, but she didn't want to visit.

'Innocents' sounded so familiar. The innocents. Now I know it referred to King Herod's killing of his own three sons in Judea in 7 BC and 4 BC, because he feared they would one day divest him of his power, but I didn't know that then and I had no desire to keep googling. We left the hotel room, stored our luggage, and started walking west towards the city centre, passing a medieval palace and a café that I'd forgotten was there, but looked unchanged. We took seats at a small round table facing a narrow pavement where well-dressed women with children or small dogs were passing by. My daughter said she was hungry and I ordered her a coffee with hot milk and a tartine, without asking if that's what she wanted because I thought she wouldn't know she wanted it. As she ate, I smoked one of the last cigarettes in my pack and snapped pictures of her on my phone. I've never needed to look at them in order to recall this breakfast and I can picture it now: the bright, hot walls to one side of me and between us the coffee cups they'd always had at this place, her finger around the jam knife and the butter and the bread and how she wiped away the crumbs, which had got stuck between the marble tabletop and its thin brass edge, or fell on the pavement where tiny reckless birds snapped them up.

She said it was the best thing she'd ever eaten and I remember the look on her face exactly. I can feel the sun on my back and the taste of the hot coffee in my mouth when I think about it. It wasn't only the fact of being with her, just her and me, and it wasn't just the promise of the hot sunny day; it was also a day when my existence was still intact.

Yes, something had begun to happen, a measure of chaos and dissolution had already cast itself across the world, bringing with it a sense that nothing that had been self-evident could be taken as such anymore, but this rupture hadn't quite reached me yet, not as more than a barely discernible whiff of rot that I could still put out of my mind, so far. I still possessed the blind trust of someone who has never had to fear for her own or anyone else's humanity. I still put trust in language and the word. I thought I was safe.

It was only shortly after ten when we got to the neighbourhood around Les Halles and approached the address I'd typed into Google Maps. The pavement had been swept and washed and in spite of the heat there was still a hint of morning in the air. We crossed a pedestrianised road that has a McDonald's and a KFC on it and went on to the fountain where I used to hang out when I was my daughter's age. She had been looking for a pair of trousers in a style that had been popular then and which had come back in fashion, and when she spotted some second-hand shop across the square she stopped, wanting to go in and browse. I asked her to call me when she was finished.

A second later I was on the square, looking out over it. I was overcome with embarrassment: imagine having been so attached to this place. Around the fountain it was empty. Only a few people were sitting on its pale flagstones: a couple of tourists, two women in niqaabs and a man reading the newspaper. Further off, a group of young guys were standing, heads close together, talking about dealing or fencing drugs, I presumed. The fountain itself was dingy and the two nymphs in bas-relief had been tagged with black spray paint. The raised fount in the middle was shut off and where water had once trickled now had pigeons pecking at an accumulation of rubbish.

I checked my phone to see which direction to go, but when I saw the line between the blue dot marking my position and the green one marking my destination I realised I was already there: the address I'd typed in was some ten metres away. I started walking; even though I was so close, I still kept an eye on the screen. I walked diagonally across the open square until I saw a street sign with the poet's name on a post right beside it.

I'd never suspected that this was what Place Joachim du Bellay was, a patch of empty asphalt between the fountain and the pedestrianised road with the fast food chains. Once a man had come up to me there and punched me in the face, then he'd walked off as if nothing had happened.

Aside from the sign there was nothing, not even a bench, but this was what had once been Place des Innocents. Here lay the cemetery visited by Roberval and other Reformists that evening in April 1560. It was there that they had been discovered – it may have been 18 April, judging by a piece of information about a Protestant burial that is said to have taken place there then. By this point, Calvinism had spread and the persecution of French Huguenots had escalated. A person spying on the gathering had called in reinforcements and more and more clustered, encircling the men. Jean-François de la Rocque de Roberval managed to make a run for it, but was quickly ensnared by the crowd.

I remembered the list of the most tortuous ways to die that my daughter had read aloud to me the night before when we'd been lounging around with our phones in the hotel room. Being beaten to death by a mob wasn't among them.

I wondered where she'd been when she'd found out that he'd been killed, and what she thought. She must have had an easier time than I did imagining the scene. And news of his death must have reached her, somehow. I couldn't imagine it any other way.

I turned around and walked back to the fountain and caught sight of a sign right beneath one of the sculptures:

Fontaine des Innocents. I couldn't remember having seen it before. I sat on the fountain's edge and took out my notebook and tried to remember how it had felt to sit there when I was young. The person I had been then. I'd already talked to my daughter about it, about everyone who gathered there, the mix of people and what it had meant to me, but I didn't know if it interested her.

I'd jotted a few lines on a page in my notebook and sensed somebody watching me. I looked up and saw her sitting at a distance, holding a shopping bag in one hand. She was smiling.

'How's it going? Can we go now?'

'Yes,' I said. 'I'm almost done. Just one last thing.'

She shuffled closer to me on the stone ledge and waited for me to finish writing. I put my notebook back in my bag and took out my phone to text a friend. I wrote that I had found the place where Roberval had been killed and that it happened to be the place in Paris I had visited the most. I swiped through the emojis until I found a bomb, which I appended to the message, next to the usual heart. Then I got up and took my daughter by the hand and we left.

I don't think about that day as often anymore. It's so hot here now, too. The past weeks have been almost unbearable. Animals appear more often during the day, moose and deer descend from the forest on the hill to lick salt from the road and nibble on what is left of the greenery down here.

It's early, four in the morning, as I'm writing this, but I can already tell that it will be even hotter today. I woke up only a short while ago, got out of bed as quietly as I could so as not to wake the others, came out here and sat down as I have done every morning this summer. It's not dark outside but neither has it started to get light. I've pushed open each and every veranda window in order to feel the air, which is heavy and thick with moisture and heat, and so I'll be able to hear the new local rooster crow in about an hour. If I turn around and look through the open doors I can see my husband and children sleeping. The book we're reading, *The Lion, the Witch and the Wardrobe* by C.S. Lewis, is open on the floor – the children in the story have stepped out of the wardrobe and into a land of eternal winter; they have just found out that the fawn that saved Lucy has been captured by the queen's secret police for this act, for protecting a human, but also that the trees in the forest will protect them.

It's just a matter of knowing which trees.

On the table in front of me, my books and papers sit next to the computer along with the sunflowers I brought in yesterday. They're the only flowers we have left here now, the only ones that can endure this drought. They slump in the vase, half-dead, their slim yellow petals drooping over the dark disk florets – but it's only four o'clock, five past now, and soon this will have changed.

I hadn't thought it would take this long. I thought I'd be done as soon as the worst had passed, that I'd finish as soon as I got beyond it, but instead I've continued and every now and then it's like I'm beginning again, even though I've been doing this for so long. I have the last of Marguerite de Navarre's stories still to read and yesterday we drove to the petrol station to pick up a biography of her that I'd ordered from an antiquarian bookseller online. I unpacked it as soon as we were in the car driving home and the first page I opened to, in a chapter on the symbolism surrounding Navarre, I read that her flower wasn't the ox-eye daisy, *margerit* in Swedish, but the sunflower, a heliotrope. *Le tournesol*, as it is called in French.

They still look like they're sleeping in the vase, but I can see the sky reddening now and that the sun is making its way above the treetops; its rays have already reached the ditch by the road and are shimmering on the grass by the trampoline on a neighbour's property. Right there is where the dew still collects at night, even though the ground is so dry and the groundwater is running out. In this moment, the blades of grass look unreal, like fine illuminated brushstrokes.

I notice that I don't want it to end. I don't want to add a full stop. Finally, I can see it so clearly, I can see what this writing is. I see myself and my fear of what lies beyond it, after the end. How arduous it seems. It feels shameful to think of it and of how much I'd wanted to write something that benefitted someone else, something that would be pure and clear and full of meaning.

The sun is higher now, but it takes a little longer for it to reach in here, flashing on the wax cloth on the table and rousing the flowers from their dark sleep. Soon they will raise their heads and open up to the light, untroubled, as though nothing had been difficult and as though they'd simply been waiting for this moment. And when this happens I'm going to get up and walk into the other room and lie down next to the others and fall back asleep.

The quotes from *The Heptameron of the Tales of Margaret, Queen of Navarre* are taken from George Saintsbury's translation of the *Authentic Text of M. Le Roux de Lincy*, from the 1894 edition printed for the Society of English Bibliophilists, London, and reissued digitally as a Project Gutenberg e-book.

The quotes from *La Cosmographie Universelle* and *La Grande Insulaire* are taken from Elizabeth Boyer's *A Colony of One*.

Quotes from *The Book of the City of Ladies* by Christine Pizan are taken from Rosalind Brown-Grant's translation, published by Penguin in 1999.

Author's Note

Like the narrator of this book, I, too, was captivated by the story of the bear woman without really knowing anything about her. I'd heard that she was stranded on a desert island, had experienced appalling things and survived by killing bears. This was all I knew, and when I started trying to find out more, it turned out there wasn't much to know.

The historical account of her is a web of assumptions and guesswork held together by legends and small fragments of facts. We know very little about the bear woman, just as we know very little about many other women in history. Only a few details can be seen as substantiated, and what I've imagined about her, as described in these pages, is for the most part grounded in these, or originates with them in some way. I wanted to stick close to the few available facts and their concomitant assumptions – not because it wouldn't be good or right to spin fiction out of thin air, but because it became a method for me, a way of writing that arose from the blank space and the great silence that is women's history.

Of the contemporary sources, the writing of André Thevet – a renowned traveller and member of the royal court – are the most abundant, and the only ones with a direct claim to truth. Thevet writes that the bear woman, Marguerite, is a close relative of Jean-François de la Rocque de Roberval, but does not specify how they are related and doesn't give her family name. So it's not entirely clear what her name is, her family ties aren't clear and neither is her age. I've imagined that she was born around 1523, and so was about nineteen when she was dumped on the island. The fact that she quickly became pregnant and could endure such severe hardship speaks to her being young, as does the relatively certain assumption that Roberval was her guardian. But this guardianship is only presumed because no young noblewoman would have been sent on a journey like this without her family.

It is most likely that she was an orphan and Roberval was her guardian. It is certain that she was of noble birth, had a maidservant, was Protestant and was very unusual in that she had been taught to read and write despite being a woman. On this journey to the New World, she brought along Damienne as her chaperone and the banned New Testament. She had the book with her on the island and said that it was what had saved her, having it there to read.

The timeline is also verified thanks to documentation from Roberval's expedition: they left La Rochelle harbour aboard *La Vallentyne* on 16 April 1542, arrived at St John's on 8 June, and the island a bit later.

In André Thevet's interview with her, Marguerite describes her conditions, what happened and in which order and approximately when. Some things aren't spelled out, such as her marriage. Thevet calls the man Marguerite's husband, and we can assume that they entered into marriage through handfasting – otherwise she wouldn't have mentioned the child she had borne. In all that he writes, Thevet meticulously omits her husband's name and the sex of their offspring. None of the contemporary sources even come close to revealing the man's identity, which speaks to him coming from a family that was not to be dishonoured or provoked. Some names of the nobleman who joined Roberval are recorded, but oddly enough the full passenger lists have since vanished.

In addition to writings from the French Renaissance, I have relied on Elizabeth Boyer's book *A Colony of One*, which takes an indepth look at many assumptions and refutes a number of theories still in circulation, such as Quirpon Island being the place where Marguerite was deposited, her being the same Marguerite de la Rocque who signed a document of Faith and Homage in Amboise in 1536, and that she and Roberval were siblings.

While she was conducting research in Roberval in the 1970s, Boyer found out that unfortunately the chateau's archive had been destroyed.

Boyer went on to speculate that Marguerite's father was probably Roberval's cousin, his name Odet or Ordet, who died in 1541. If this is the case, Marguerite hadn't been under his guardianship for very long when he punished her for her immorality. No other potential underlying motives behind her disembarkation are known, but we do know that she survived and returned to France in late 1544.

Elizabeth Boyer determined that, after the Norse, Marguerite was the first European to establish a lasting colony in North America. Whereas the explorers sent out by royal decree had failed in their mission, she did everything that setting up a colony entails and maintained it for over two years. Yet she remains anonymous. Like many other readers, I can feel indignant over her not being a part of our historiography, but really, the question is how could she have been when she was barely even allowed to be part of her own time? If she had made herself known or tried to take Roberval to court upon her return to France, she could well have been charged with illicit sexual relations and heresy, instead of getting the redress that we might feel she deserved. We might wish for her historic achievement to have been acknowledged – but for her this could have been life-threatening.

Most of all, I hope that she became a teacher at a girl's school, as Marguerite de Navarre writes in her version of this story. It's a happy ending. It makes sense. But how the story actually ends is as unclear as the question of who she was and if the truth was hidden to protect her or to protect the men involved.

Karolina Ramqvist, July 2021